FRANCE BEFORE EUROPE.

BY

JULES MICHELET.

TRANSLATED FROM THE FRENCH.

"LES JUGES SERONT JUGÉS."

BOSTON:
ROBERTS, BROTHERS.
1871.

CONTENTS.

TO MY TRANSLATOR.

Florence, February 26th.

It is a great pleasure for me that the translation of a book, which is of some importance in my eyes, should have been undertaken by so enlightened a mind as yours, and one who has so well and clearly caught my thought and the form in which I express it. The correction of the proofs by one whom I value and esteem, makes this translation unique and precious in every point of view to me and to all.

J. Michelet.

PREFACE TO THE FIRST EDITION.

When the Emperor of Russia received the news of the battle of Wörth (our first defeat), he could not repress his transports of joy. He was at dinner, and to relieve his feelings, he tossed off, in old German fashion, a great goblet of wine, and then threw it up to the ceiling, whence it fell and shivered to atoms. The tumbler out of which he had drunk at such a moment could not be defiled by further use.

This barbaric joy is the synonym of the serious phrase made use of by the German workmen in their petition for peace. The Czar thought their prophecy was already accomplished. "This war will result in the victory of Russia over Germany."

Over Europe and over the world! Germany, by exhausting itself in destroying France, opens a royal road to the Tartar Russian legions.

The report of this toast, and of this broken tumbler, was not agreeable to Russia's friend. Count Bismarck sighed. His ingenious operation of chloroforming England while he executed France might be disturbed by the sound. England, anxious about Turkey, might suddenly be roused, and thus guess the secret treaty, which the said Bismarck had signed with the Czar in July against English interests in the East. The cracked glass would make a slit or opening through which light might dawn on the English Government; it must be, therefore, immediately corked up—calked, patched over. To succeed in this what flatteries must be made use of to the gentlemen and officers with the Prussian armies, to the newspaper correspondents, and what compliments, what confidences, what dinners to the reporters! At last, all the right-thinking, and even all the dangerous-thinking, classes were sufficiently acted upon, and England fell asleep again for two months more, till the 1st of November.

Russia, which, in time of peace, has an army of 700,000 men, doubled her artillery last July. In that boreal realm of snow and silence there are no sounds or echoes—at least, at the commencement of events you hear nothing.

But what is not generally known is, that Russia, after a fashion, is a popular government. It understands how, by the application of certain violent goads, its barbarous masses can be stirred up. After Sedan, after Metz, the Czar thought it right to make an appeal to his people. The white bear opened its huge throat, and obtained an awful roar, as echo from that human sea. That race is as mobile as the ocean. Our workers of the West are sedentary races, the Russian is a vagrant. It is only the weight of an iron yoke which forces him to be a labourer; he would from choice be a boatman, a coachman, a travelling carpenter, or a pedlar. The monotony of the climate and of the landscape make him anxious to change the scene. This desire for change was felt in '53; there had been an intention to go south for the anniversary of the fall of Constantinople (1453), but instead, the Russian was taken to Poland, although Poland had been already devoured as dry as a bone. Some day he will be led into Germany.

To encourage the enthusiasm of his people, the Czar informed the journalists of St. Petersburg, and of Moscow, "Prussia is Russophile; Prussia is with me" (10th November).

This statement displeased Europe, saddened M. de Bismarck, but was a subject of rejoicing in Russia itself. A concert of wild beasts arose as in a menagerie at feeding-time. From the furious Katkoffs to the most charming damsels, there arose a cry, "Long live the Czar!" Innocent girls wrote to their companions, "How delightful—how great is the Emperor! at a bound all Russia has risen to her feet. What an admirable sight! Glory to God!"

The shouts which reached our ears through these truthful voices spoke of invasion, and warned Europe, but they disturbed Bismarck so much that, through his dear correspondents and his world of newspapers, he dared make a counter-statement in reply as strange as it was facetious. "Russia has adopted a peace policy;

Russia is disgusted with standing armies, is envious of the results of the German landwehr, and will in future only think of defensive armies." Only defensive? 500,000 young men were called out in January '71, to add to the 700,000 soldiers she had before. In all 1,200,000 or 1,300,000: that is the number stated in a quasi-official Russian newspaper. But, as this newspaper is also often made use of to deceive Europe, I trust yet more to private letters, which all speak of an impending general movement in Russia. Russia, they say, is armed and ready to march. Where? Who knows? Is it for poor weak Turkey, or for an occupation of the Wallachian Provinces? Who can believe either rumour? No, Russia is on her march westwards.

In his note of the 1st November, the Czar, giving a flourish of trumpets to rouse Russia, even more than to startle Europe, proclaimed that he considered himself no longer bound by the Treaty of 1856 guaranteed by all Europe. He asserted the liberty of doing what he pleased. England opened her eyes, and remonstrated against this slap in the face. "Be so good as to tell me why you thus attack *me*, an entirely inoffensive person?"

"I will tell you in London," said the Czar, meekly; adding, jocosely, "I will tell you what it is: Turkey is armed to the teeth, and so strong that at any moment I might be attacked in the Black Sea, and—I am afraid."

Where is France? Where is the sword which, in the Crimean war, according to the acknowledgment of an English nobleman, saved England three times? To-day England is alone, and behind her are the piratical privateers of the United States, which, like a swarm of gnats, will harass and sting English commerce in all the seas.

There is Austria, to be sure. The other day, according to Benedek, it had a million of soldiers. But Bismarck is beforehand: he manipulates that invalid empire. The Diet refuses funds for the war, and listens to the magic utterance, "The Danube is German—the Danube must belong to Austria."

But what of Russia and all the Slaves on the shores of that river? How will Bismarck settle the question? To how many people has Bismarck promised the Danube?

First and foremost, he placed Prussia there as a sentinel. A Hohenzollern at Bucharest, near the famous mouths of the Danube! Before Sadowa, he said to German patriots, "The Danube is yours—it is Germany." In 1870 he mesmerized England by saying that Turkey was the watchman and guardian of that gate of the Danube. To Russia what did he say? That he would support Russia in the East, in the Black Sea. But, as regards that Sea, the question is, who is there to hold the key of Europe? Who will be the keeper of the gate to open and shut the Danube—to confine Germany, which is always seeking an outlet there?

Russia, with its masses, rises up to-day to confront Bismarck, and to recall to him their agreement.

Russia deserves well at his hands. She has served him as Napoleon *III. (fool) served him before Sadowa.*

She said, "Go; you are safe. Throw all Germany on France,—I am responsible for the rest of the world." To put Bismarck at his ease, Russia has intimidated Italy and Denmark, and has barred their way.

Now, however, Russia appears—makes claims. How will Bismarck satisfy this giant mendicant? Can he say, "Come again, at a more convenient season?" His methods are always the same. He mystified the Emperor in 1866, England in 1870,—doubtless Russia in 1871.

The German patriots, the German professors and literati, that estimable learned but chimerical class, who have so imposed their opinion on Germany, have neglected no means to alarm nations, and to warn them they aspire to universal empire. From Holland to Switzerland, from Copenhagen to Bucharest, all is, or will be, German. Courland, Livonia, abandoning Russia, will make the Baltic German. This is their Utopia, to which, on November 26th, at the opening of their Diet, they immolated to Bismarck the liberties of their country,—yet more, the mourning and the tears of Germany, exhausted by its victories.

These profound politicians answer those who say that Bismarck deceives the whole world, "Yes; the whole world, but not *us*. You will see. He is quick, agile in his movements. Look at his clever trick at Vienna, how sharp! and his back-handed thrust at England. What a wall against Russia! Yesterday he was half-Russian, to-day he is wholly German." How is it you so blind yourselves? You see without seeing, you know without comprehending. Do you forget the terrible marriage between Prussia and Russia? It is so close, that between them treaties are unnecessary. The league of July 10th was superfluous.

Prussia, half-Slave, was the State that, in the last century, proposed the Thyestian banquet, at which Poland was devoured, and her blood was drunk. Will she be able to sever herself from that fatal communion? She has always been faithful to it,—she has found her share hard to swallow, bitter, and indigestible. Her enemy is within her. She needs Russia too—especially when the hour comes (perchance to-morrow) when Germany will wake, and come out of her dream—the dream of her present intoxication, in which the idea of being united as One has made her forget all else. But to be *united*, one must first *Be*. The day when she wills To be, her tyrant Prussia will appeal to Russia. Austria is too tottering to give her support. Through Prussia alone, Russia will hold down her Slaves, silence her Germans.

Even now, while France is yet struggling, how coolly Prussia treats Germany. The Prince of Saxony arrested, the German correspondent at Versailles driven to suicide: do not such facts reveal from what feudal heights Prussia looks at Germany. The arrest of Jacoby, the bastard constitution violated from the first by the imprisonment for two years of its free-speaking deputies:—does not that attest what I say?

To me, you German professors, you are, I assure

you, a wonderful anomaly. You live in a magic world of proud and learned dreams. Seeing you so civilized, so industrious, and in every way so fruitful in comparison with that barren and iron Prussia, you say to yourselves, "Great Germany will absorb Prussia, as Italy absorbed Piedmont. What is Prussia but a military organization? Without us she is nothing. The genius which illumines Berlin is of the Rhine, Suabian, Saxon. Even in militarism, the Prussians live on borrowed intellect. Their great commander is a Dane. We surround, we overwhelm Prussia with the power of arts and of civilization. If she thinks, if she governs, it is by us."

Vain and fallacious hope! It is just because Prussia is inferior and barren, dry, unyielding, that her rough kernel will never be assimilated or absorbed by Germany.

You speak of Prussia as if there was an individual Prussia to be grasped, as if it had life, and as if your life could exist and act with its life. But what is Prussia? Are there Prussians? I doubt it. Their names are all Slave, Swedish, Danish, Swiss, Russian. It is an absorbing frame, a stomach and claws like a polypus; but it has no body.

In this solemn and serious moment, while Russia is on her march, while Germany is worn out and exhausted by her victories, while England deliberates (paralysed or betrayed), while Austria is powerless to arm, while kings veil their faces not to see the coming storm, farewell, ye monarchies—arise, ye people!

A workman appeals to all the workers in the world, and adjures them to form the armed league of peace.

That which the German craftsman says wisely, the English workman manifests by his monster demonstrations. At this moment of danger in which we are placed by the Prusso-Russian militarism, it behoves the great class of workers, the laborious, industrious, productive nations to arm, not for France alone, but for themselves—for all who are producers against all who are destroyers—Life against Death.

Let us look down on this bloody Europe. What do we behold? In the west are looms, workshops, factories, the great agricultural manufactures, the men who produce, the creators of the universal wealth of the world. From the east come the men who destroy.

But we, say the Germans, are here. Poland was once a barrier against Russia, but now it will be Germany.

The unity of such a nation would in truth be a great power. But is it a sincere unity? Is unity union? Is Hanover German with all her heart? How reluctantly has Bavaria been forced into this unity.

Germans, do you know how the Slaves hate you? Your inveterate hatred against us has made you overlook or forget it. But he who runs may read it. The long utilisation made by the Germans (in Courland) of the Russian people has sown the seed of a deep and bitter hate. The stewards of the noblemen, the officials of the Czar, are generally German. It is an unfailing proverb that, if a man is flogged in Russia, the stick is held by a German.

Do you think you can trust to these people for gratitude? Can you trust to the faithful ally of your greatest enemy?

Your civilization, your industrial progress, your superiority in the arts of peace, are precisely what in a war with Russia will make your inferiority. She fights with men of such slight individual value that she can be lavish of their lives. What is the value of an European, an Englishman, a Frenchman, a German? Much, if you consider what he can produce—what he can earn. How much does a Russian peasant produce? how much does he earn? Russia has but a poor stake to risk—and you?

An industrious people, devoted to peaceful occupations, to produce and to create, can tear itself away from them in a great popular movement, such as we have lately seen. But it is against the grain. And if the war is a long one, it weighs heavily on it. Are you not wearied of this one?

It is true you have been dazzled. An impious whisper was muttered to you. Destroy France. But that is impossible. France can never be destroyed. One of our men said the other day: "The war will begin in the spring."

When you have crushed Paris (which is yet doubtful) there will always remain France.

Pillage and requisitions have roused the peasant. He is now aware that whether he fights or whether he yields he is ruined. Yesterday's harvest, the vintage, his much loved cow, his oxen, have all been taken from him. He who loses all this, finds,—can you guess what ?—that which had been lost for a time, the warlike instincts of his fathers, the soldiers of liberty. The peasant has been ruined at the moment when he was being enriched by the new outlets of the south and the west, when he was hoarding money and acquiring land. In August, 1870, he was absorbed in this work. It would be folly to think he desired war. Had it been even a victorious war, it would have disturbed and, perchance, arrested his progress in proprietorship.

Our frontier departments were, it is true, irritated by the insults of the Prussians, who, since Sadowa were full of bravado and defiance. I have never seen men more arrogant. The very earth seemed to them unworthy of them. I heard them in Switzerland, in 1867, say over and over again : "After Sadowa, Paris : next year we will take it." After the Great Exhibition, when we had received them with our best hospitality, they took away with them drawings of our fortifications, and printed a Military and Topographical Manual of how to undertake the siege of Paris.

The Emperor Napoleon had shamefully endured the swallowing up of Hanover, Hesse, Nassau, Frankfort, in Prussia, and had been deaf to their cries. But Prussia defied him beyond all bounds. He had at least striven to shelter Bavaria, Würtemberg, and to prevent their sliding down into the bloody gulf with the rest of Germany. What says Bavaria now? and her thirty thousand bereaved families, and twenty-nine thousand widows?

For us, for our part we have always desired the real unity of Germany, a real voluntary unity, not this savage, violent, forced unity. A war to obtain her liberties would have been approved as just by us; a war which would have had freedom for its object. If we were indignant at the war, it was because we felt we had been swindled. Our Government had extorted a vote on the plea of assuring peace, and when it had been obtained, war was declared. We knew that all the industrial part of the nation was averse to it, and even more, was, in an economical sense, quite contrary to it. I was the first, I think, who published a letter in the newspapers to protest against the snare which had been laid for us.

Now, the peasant who was yesterday but an ox amid his furrows, is a lion. Twenty-six million peasants. To these add ten million craftsmen, and brave ones, if we may judge by Paris workmen. Of this agricultural population of twenty-six millions, twenty millions are landholders: four millions of families, and therefore twenty millions of individuals. It is the widest basis a nation ever had. A thousand years of struggle will not exhaust its blood. A peasant on his own land, and rooted to it by a thousand ties, is renewed, reinvigorated on it, increases a hundredfold in strength and persistence, and will be firm and invincible in its defence.

Happily for Europe it is so. In the future impending war Europe needs France. Europe will rejoice to see France is so tough, and to find her grown greater through this fierce strife, and to know she is so warlike and will be so formidable against the coming barbaric invasion.

This, in two words, is the subject of this book.

Workers, creators, indefatigable producers, stand together as one people. Preserve for the world the sacred source which produces all its wealth.

I appeal and invoke, in an European congress, all men who work, all men who rise to work, as I do before daylight as I write this to-day, 1st of January, 1871. I appeal to Englishmen, Frenchmen, Belgians, Dutch, Swiss. I appeal to Germans.

I invoke both worlds. I appeal to young America. Let her justify our hope and be deaf to all petty interests, free from all mean revenges, vowed to the great cause of human progress, closely allied to the civilized West and to the cause of freedom, for which but yesterday she so nobly fought and conquered.

I speak for the world more even than for France. France will save herself. But will the world be saved while it hesitates and is divided? At this supreme moment I call on all to unite for defence and to arm. The enemy is on us.

PREFACE TO THE SECOND EDITION.

I HAD finished this book at the end of December. How much has happened in a month! What cruel tragedies have darkened this pitiless January. And at the end of it, what a blow! . . . But we are not overwhelmed.

The bitterest winter which has been known for years intensified the war, and made it more intolerable. The cold was nineteen degrees below freezing in the Vosges. Our enemies, almost countless in number, and so infinitely superior to us in resources of all kinds, and well fed, took a rude advantage of the season, of our destitution, and of our numberless miseries. Instead of success softening them, it irritated them into fury. How many "franc-tireurs" have they not shot! We have all heard of their attacks upon peasants, of the burning of villages, and of the outrages upon ambulances and the killing of French surgeons. All this has been proved by a regular inquiry, so circumstantially, that they cannot themselves deny it.

Hitherto, the world has seen nothing like this. It has been beheld by all with horror and loathing. The very excess of our sufferings, the heroism of our resistance, have surprised and touched all. What a revulsion of public feeling in Europe! I can dare to say now,—No more neutrals in Europe. An American said to me this morning, "Yesterday, we were Germans; to-day, we are all French."

A great city of two millions of souls, which it was impossible to feed, where the duration of the provisions had been calculated, and were known to be at an end, was wantonly bombarded at the very moment that famine obliged it to surrender.

And in what manner was it bombarded? With the same science of terrorism which has been so ably followed in this war, sparing the walls, aiming at the inhabitants. The German maps of Paris, drawn in '67, directed them admirably. Numberless shells were fired on the portions of the city occupied by schools, colleges, and hospitals. The peaceful Paris, of children and professors and of learned men, the Jardin des Plantes, and the Institute, is as a world apart from the world of action. I remember, in 1815, the respect with which Alexander of Russia, and the other kings, guided by M. de Humboldt, visited the Institute and the Jardin des Plantes. To-day, it is a different kind of visit. A shell fell on the venerable houses of Cuvier, Geoffroy St. Hilaire, close to his widow's bedside, a woman eighty-four years of age. And why all this? Paris was eating the actual seed reserved for this next year's sowing, the public authorities were selling it in the market, the end was approaching, and every one knew it. There had been no firing during this terrible winter. Bercy had been burned, and with it all the wine. Nothing was left to oppose to the cold, nothing remained with which to animate or restore courage and ardour. But Paris was in this moment truly great. In the future let us never forget it.

The neighbouring heights which command its forts had not been occupied in August by the Regent; in September, the enemy took them, and during four months armed them at his leisure, and connected these positions with good batteries, which were covered, walled, and casemated, from whence he could fire in all security. A terrible girdle, which was built slowly and securely, while Paris was preparing itself and arming for her defence. In December and in January, that girdle was closely clasped with double and treble clasps. Behind it an emperor was made. Behind it, according to that part of the *Times* which is edited at Versailles, the Prussian can grin and defy the Parisian. Is not the latter in truth *in extremis*. Lions themselves are weakened by the privation of food, by vigils, by febrile agitation. An increasing starvation must have disarmed and exhausted the city. Well, on the 19th of January, this people march on Versailles. These inexperienced novices, these unformed legions of artists, literati, artist workers, a total of men with little muscular strength, accustomed to the arts of peace, rush at the stronghold and best guarded portion of Versailles. They wished to see that Emperor with their own eyes, and for that purpose sought to penetrate that enormous "carapace" of stone, iron, and fire. At one spring they take St. Cloud and its thundering batteries. For nine hours they keep possession of it beneath its storm of balls; it is taken and retaken: there was great alarm felt at Versailles, and Marly was attacked. It was during that deadly struggle that the news came of the defeat of Le Mans, when our generals put an end to all.

If the stone walls were harder than human breast, the effort was no less a sublime one. It was a struggle of spiritual against material powers.

Learn, ye nations, from such a spectacle in what consists true greatness, and revere France!

I have read many histories. But I have never read of so brave, yet humane a revolution, so generous towards its barbarous enemies, and shewing such clemency even to treason.

Above all so unanimous. That is its great feature. For if a small number of fanatics desired (contrary to all good sense or possible hope) to rush and fight again, that could not be called a division in the principles of the camp. On both sides were firm Republicans.

It is this which Europe has seen and which decides her award. All hearts speak now for us. Our enemy knows that he has lost the moral victory. Bruised and mutilated France is still unconquered. She yet remains France, formidable, strong, and greater than before.

But this strength, cannot it be employed against herself? That is the last hope of the enemy.

The bitterest trial, it is true, has yet to be undergone. The Elections, while the victor still occupies the country, amidst traitors, or what is worse, cowards.

Those who, from error or weakness, in voting "yes" brought on the war, and who without foresight have ruined us, those will now have been taught better, I am sure. They are warned. Altogether let us be only One.

Feb. 1, 1871.

FRANCE BEFORE EUROPE.

CHAPTER I.

THE ILLUSIONS OF BIARRITZ.

1865-6.

THE historians of the future will find a difficulty in making themselves believed as to a matter which, though it seems ridiculous, is still perfectly true. In this nineteenth century the most important events of the world —those which were, in fact, its destiny—were treated, discussed, negotiated, on a basis as fantastic and unreal as the adventures of the *Arabian Nights*. Serious affairs of statesmanship, in their most critical phase, were set adrift and floated between the romantic glitter of the mines of Mexico and the Fata Morgana of the Rhine.

It certainly was a great triumph of state-craft to induce Napoleon, worn, aged, and more undecided and fanciful than ever, so repeatedly to leave the capital where he might have retained a little good sense, to go and dream on the isolated shores of Biarritz, near the castles in the air of the land of Cervantes. Those domestic influences which weigh so masterfully at the decline of life had, of course, a great deal to do with it: the faithful remembrance which some persons have of the home of their youth, and the pleasant and natural opportunities of occasionally returning to it, which were offered by Biarritz.

Biarritz is famous for shipwrecks of all kinds. Sailors who have been round the world say they have never seen anything like the terrible swell of the sea which from the N.W. rolls into a gulf of unfathomable depth at that point, and then rises high to strike St. Jean de Luz, half drowned as it already is. The Basques of this shore are a wild, giddy, adventurous race. It was one of their games, during their feasts and holidays, to make their boats skim and dance on this foaming whirlpool. The coast is nicknamed "The Coast of Lunatics." The wives of these Basque mariners, more extravagant than their husbands, often during their voyages north, were wont to celebrate on the sandy plains at home the witch-revels of the middle ages, when Sabbat was held to consult the Evil One.

Weirdly-shaped hills of strange outline indicate how near is Spain—that country so rife in falsehoods, and which shines with a pseudo-lustre from its golden past, from its mines, its famous galleons, and the tawny glitter derived from its lost provinces. In the evenings of Biarritz, with their glowing sunsets, how easy to revive these ancient visions, and restore Spain, Mexico, Vera Cruz. To make the dream more utterly wild and intangible, the idea was evoked of establishing an Austrian Montezuma in a resuscitated Mexican Empire. What a strange house of cards! It is more than probable that one of the architects was that fairy Austrian who was the delight of that court by her singular and fantastic whims.

But the house of cards began to totter in 1865. The Mexican-Austrian was oblivious of his maker; his pretty young bride had irritated Biarritz. It was a fortunately chosen moment, therefore, when the incarnate Spirit of Craft, coming from the north, appeared on the scenes to plot against Austria.

"False as water," says Shakspeare. How admirably those words suit the two who are conversing on that beach. One is from the Baltic, with its deep and deceitful quicksands deserted by the sea, but where it is possible to sink and be drowned on dry land; the other comes from the dull low tides of Holland, with its treacherous earth, and reminds one of its sad sea-gulls by his leaden mournful look.

What are they speaking about? Each hopes to deceive the other. Nothing is written down in black and white; but it is folly to think the tempter offered nothing, promised nothing, or that he did not bait his hook. It is certain now that he did promise much.

The Emperor, whatever may since have been said,

was free to act as he pleased. He could have checkmated his antagonist. He had not more than 28,000 men in Mexico; for France that was a trifle: he was sure of England by the free-trade treaty: the United States were still occupied in their great war. To atone to France for his Mexican blunder, he wished to obtain some advantage on the Rhine. The Wizard of the North made him believe that he held the Rhine in his hand, and tempted him with Cologne and Coblentz.

"But what will Germany say?"

"Sire, have I not the German patriots on my side? That is the best of it. I led them to Schleswig; I will throw them on the Danube. The Danube must become German; it must be open to the Black Sea and to the East. I will intoxicate them by a victory over Austria, and they will let go the Rhine." All this was spoken freely, frankly, with the open honesty of a straightforward German, of a rough and ready soldier, with the military out-spokenness which belongs to a diplomatic Cuirassier. Add to this the easy, confidential footing inseparable from a seaside life and the trust which one invalid reposes in another. The Cuirassier is in bad health, so is the Emperor. Bismarck would die if it were not for Biarritz; but every year he goes there for the baths and to attend to his health. There only is he really well; there only does he forget his state cares. There, if one could get at him, one would find "by Jove" he sincerely says all he thinks. Deuce take diplomacy! he is as open as the day; he wears his heart on his sleeve. His rude soldierly aspect speaks for him; how would it be possible for him to deceive? His rough visage is an invaluable mask for the incomparable actor. It is the more so because, in addition to its ugliness, it is humorous, has a certain caricatured resemblance to a fire-eater about it, which delights King William and his junkers. The studied photographs lately taken of him partly conceal this aspect beneath the vizor of his spiked helmet; but the earlier ones, more truthful, reveal him better in the vigorous grotesqueness which is so useful to him, with eyes upraised to heaven, where he sees a transcendent vision—the German Fatherland, a Germany which absorbs the entire world.

Why not? Teutons in their credulity find this expansion natural and simple. What is *not* the German fatherland? Holland, Denmark, Sweden, Switzerland, England, France are included in it; the Baltic and the Black Sea are German; does not the Black Sea receive the Danube, which is a German river? The United States, by the progress of emigration, are German. In Europe three sentinels answer for it, three Hohenzollerns; one at the mouth of the Danube, one by the Straits of Gibraltar, one by Kehl on the Rhine.

The Cuirassier is a poet. What a vast poem! what a genius for fiction! And all this was readily swallowed by him whose covetous greed blinded him to realities. With him how easy was the task of deception. Forwards, bold guardsman, forwards in the realm of fiction.

Be the Ossian of Berlin, the Ossian of Biarritz. King William sees himself a modern Barbarossa; Napoleon wears the glory of Napoleon the Great.

The Great! but which is the Great—the uncle or the nephew? After all, the uncle did little. "The Rhine, which I give you here, is but a commencement. Your eagles will alight first on Coblentz, will then take wing from thence towards Antwerp, Amsterdam, London. Their beaks will be sharpened there—it will be the revenge of Waterloo. But one hemisphere is not enough. This Europe is so small. America shall yield too; is not Liberty wounded to death in her great republic? You and I, by a common effort, will crush everywhere our common enemy—Revolution."

We all know how these promises were kept after Sadowa, after the shameful service which the Emperor rendered towards Prussia, in abandoning Austria, and in accepting without a murmur the annihilation of Hanover, Hesse, Nassau, Frankfort, as well as Schleswig. Nothing now was concealed. The very day when a promise was made to respect the south (Bavaria, Würtemberg), they were forced to sign a military treaty which gave their armies to Prussia.

France was daily defied and insulted; drunken Prussians outraged us at Strasbourg. It reminds one of the poems of Renaud, where a successor of Charlemagne is profoundly asleep on the throne of France, and a stranger with a torch shaves him.

CHAPTER II.

FRENCH SYMPATHY AND HOSPITALITY.

1867.

France rejoiced at the victory of Sadowa. We were delighted to confront our old technical soldiers, the soldiers by profession, with praises of a success which was partly due to the citizen Landwehr. We would not, or could not, understand the great part taken in these victories by the permanent army of Prussia, a caste entirely devoted to war; the troops trained to the use of special arms, skilfully organized; in short, that great machine which, more than any other in the world, represents the predominance of militarism in European politics. We supposed it was simply a victory of the people conquering its unity. The lists published of the wounded of the Landwehr—lists in which were names from all civil professions: lawyers, physicians, professors, mechanics—strengthened our illusions. We were quite touched by it. We were struck by the victory of Protestant culture over barbarous Catholicism. We would not listen to those who said that the true conqueror was the needle-gun; that without that instrument and its terrible rain of fire, which suppresses all struggle, the citizen of the north would never have overcome the Austro-Hungarian army, so brave, so war-hardened, which we had learned to know by its hard-fought battles in Italy. We did not know that Austria left its army destitute and wretched, and without food for three days. We did not remember that the Italian alliance with Prussia retained a third, at least, of the Austrian army to guard Venetia and the Quadrilateral. We, unawares, had co-operated strenuously in this war. How much we did, apparently doing nothing! If Prussia needed only a small detachment to overpower the great masses of Bavaria and the west of Germany, it was because of the strange absence of our soldiers on the Rhine—the mysterious inaction of the Emperor unnerved their courage and their arms. Prussia herself avowed it in her solemn thanks to the Emperor.

What is most striking about this war is, that Germany conquered in spite of herself. She cursed the unquiet, adventurous spirit who plunged her in these dangerous enterprises. What misery at partings, as the soldiers joined their corps! what indignation, even in the officers whom we met in the trains! This great industrious country, every year more industrial, left, with intense difficulty, its occupations, its affairs, and its well-ordered life. The irritation and discontent were such that in the college where M. de Bismarck's sons were studying, their comrades, with the rudeness of their age, overwhelmed them with the invectives and reproofs which they overheard applied to their father at their homes.

The Germans call the French fickle, but how rapidly and lightly they changed after Sadowa. What a contrast! what a noisy awakening! In their hotels, their clamours, their loquacity, their bravadoes were such that English and French insisted on dining at tables apart from them, where would come also Hanoverians—men from Frankfort and the other free-towns—who saw in the Prussian victories the eternal downfall of the liberty of Germany. The great majority had forgotten this. They were blind, they were intoxicated with a passion—a most natural and legitimate one, it is true—the love, the rapture, the triumph of their unity. All people have these moments of divine delirium, and then they are blind. Italy has had hers. This frenzy, this fury of unity, has mastered her and led her to the limits of actual crime. For the sake of unity, the Ghibeline Dante appealed to the foreigner, and in Guelph Florence, Machiavelli would, to obtain this end, have accepted any aid, however monstrous, even that of the fiend, Cæsar Borgia. At such moments in the unity of one's country one would embrace the unity of the world. So Italy and Germany, through Rome and the Holy Empire, in their dreams absorbed all. And as these German dreamers drink deep of every cup, they always obstinately evoke two shadows—Charlemagne, who from the Rhine governed the Empire and

France; and Frederic Barbarossa, who, they say, with Germany, held Rome and Lyons—the kingdom of Lombardy, and the kingdom of Burgundy. But why confine ourselves to this limit? Does not the German Fatherland extend itself wherever German or its dialects is spoken? Holland, Sweden, Denmark, Switzerland, Anglo-Saxon England, are they not all provinces of Germany? This mental insanity—an actual disease—is especially perceptible in the learned portions of society, professors, students, &c. I have in my hand at this moment an article in a journal of *Berlin*, which is headed, "Down with Schiller!" Schiller committed the unpardonable sin of immortalizing William Tell—a miscreant who dared to revolt against the supremacy of Germany.

Drunkenness leads to wickedness, even when it is patriotic drunkenness. German patriots had astonished us by their extreme violence against Denmark. It was then they commenced making themselves blind beasts of burden, to draw the cannons of Prussia, and to subordinate Germany to Prussia. They knew, but they persisted in not knowing, the wide barrier which separates them from the Scandinavian states, as well as from Holland and England. A faint identity of language matters little in a question of nationality. The Alsatian speaks a German patois, but does not understand German spoken a league beyond his frontier, and is not German. And if there is a country in all the world hostile by its lively individuality to all notions or customs which may be called German, it is Lorraine.

How prosperity alters people. Before Sadowa the old resentments of the Napoleonic invasions seem to have died out among people whose forefathers had twice invaded France, and who have entered twice into Paris. The one wiped out the other. But after Sadowa they forgot 1814 and 1815, and only remembered Jena: that is to say, if we would speak truly, that old feuds and hatreds of race must, after all, sooner or later, rise up with a fury, a jealousy which may be hidden for a time, but which explodes at last in those wild and causeless animosities which *we* call German quarrels.

M. de Bismarck, with his usual cynical frankness, in his last State Papers, takes the ground that between France and Germany, an eternal hatred will ever subsist, and that all good policy must always be grounded on that fact.

This atrocity would shock me less, if I did not see the care with which this hatred is taught to, and cultivated in, the young generation. Their school-books contain all which can most irritate Germans against France. Children are taught to hate and curse that which they do not even know. The other day a charming child, a little German girl of five years old, when told that her cousin was French, flushed with anger, and, stamping her tiny feet, exclaimed,—"No, not French—never French," with a shudder of horror.

What an education! In the arms of a gentle mother, on the breast of a good nurse, they breathe in, they suck enmity and hatred! In France there is nothing of the kind. Even after the bitterest, longest, most intense struggles, France feels no bitterness. France always acknowledges the merit of her adversaries. It is a memorable fact, but it is no less a fact: twenty years of bloody warfare, culminating in Waterloo, have not engrained a lasting hatred against the English. Even in 1816, France loved Walter Scott, hailed the advent of Byron. What ties of friendship, business, speculations, family connections, marriages between French and English. The greatness of the English Empire, which was first upraised, in 1763, on the ruins of France, has not bequeathed to us either envy or regret.

This is the fault, the short-coming of France. She is social, and she likes, and is interested in the outer world. She finds excellent reasons for loving, esteeming, admiring all these great nations. These manias which she manifests periodically for each and all (and which are ludicrous in their exaggeration), have, however, one good point. Each of these nations represents some excellence, some superiority in the human soul. Never did this universal good-will so display itself as after Sadowa, at a time so pregnant with trouble and defiance. I speak of the Great Exhibition of '67. That festival we gave Europe. What a welcome we gave our guests! What trust! what blind hospitality! No inn, no hotel would have sufficed for that affluence. We opened wide our houses—our hearths. We crowded ourselves in our small Parisian rooms; the master of the house would give up his best rooms to his visitors from the provinces, as from other countries, and content himself with a corner, a hole in it for himself. We suppressed doors—we would have knocked down walls, so as to enable one town to contain every one—to comprise the world. This gush of fraternity caused a great writer to say, "No more boundaries — all humanity is a brotherhood—come in all, this town is yours."

How were these advances received? I own they may have seemed odd and excessive. They were accepted dubiously, equivocally, almost ironically. Here were millionaires, Russian Princes, or English Peers, who deemed they could hire Paris as one hires an hotel, a place of entertainment, careless of all that which it is impossible to pay for, the gracious and sympathetic welcome with which Paris receives foreigners. What did they see of the town? the Boulevards, the theatres. Did they even guess at the surging fruitful Paris, that glowing manufactory of so many arts, of which Europe accepts the produce without a word. Other foreigners, poorer, more malevolent, more prying, looked at all the wonders with a forced smile, tried to be indifferent, but in spite of themselves were livid with envy.

It is dreadful to think of, but it is no less true, that these searching observers whom we led everywhere, were all the while observing and drawing our fortresses, our walls, the weak points of our fortifications. In December '67 our guests, after their return to Berlin, published a military manual, which gives in the greatest detail the topography of the suburbs of the town, its approaches, and the easy infallible method of bombarding it.

Nothing was neglected by which this military fever could be excited to frenzy. Bismarck boasts (grotesque but astute flatterer of popular passion) that he was resolved to enter Paris, armed with his pointed helmet, and he did so. This carnival entrance, in a friendly city, seemed heroic to the fanatical Germans. This strange head-dress symbolized the helmet of Arminius. By the Prusso-Russian alliance it is the helmet of Attila. We Parisians, according to our wont, smiled and jested at this, but remained faithful in our sympathies. Mine has never varied. That very year, 1867, as I concluded my most important work, the *History of France*, and in the Preface recapitulated the labours and studies which have filled my whole life, I enumerated with pleasure the various influences I had received from Germany, in my progressive mental growth, the student and literary passion—no weaker word will serve to express my feelings—with which that strong sister of our French culture had inspired me. I particularly loved its primitive genius, its virile accent, the stirring vibration of its ancient tongue, its popular wisdom in the traces which we possess of its weisthümer, of its judges, who, like the Israelites of old, found and learnt, under the great shadow of elms and poplars, so much of humanity. This mania carried me so far that I undertook the enormous task (difficult and insane as it was) to translate Grimm's book on the *Antiquities of German Law*. Grimm himself upheld, encouraged, and praised my work. How I profited by this study, and how much it developed my historical acumen, I have said and repeated in my yet unpublished Preface to my *History of France*. That Preface will be a surprise after late events. God forbid that I should efface or curtail one word of it. I would not diminish by a single word all I feel I owe to Germany, to the great and good Grimm. Would I could myself add a stone to the national monument which his nation owes him, and which it will erect to him one day.

Not I alone, not we alone, students and *literati* felt these emotions. I have said in my book called *Our Sons*, with what universal sympathy on the festival of the 4th of March, 1848, we saw amongst the flags hoisted before the Madeleine, by the deputations of the exiles of all countries, the great flag of Germany, that noble tri-colour, red, black and gold; the banner of Luther, Kant, and Fichte, Schiller, Beethoven; and beside it the graceful green tri-colour of Italy. How we welcomed them! How we prayed for the unity of those countries! God grant, we said, that we may live to see a great united Germany, an united powerful Italy. The federation of the world will be imperfect, incomplete, subject to the cruel whims, and to the unholy wars of Kings, while these two great peoples are not represented there in their majesty, adding their quota of wisdom and grace to the fraternal equilibrium of the world.

CHAPTER III.

HATRED OF FRANCE.

Why is it that the nation which hates least is hated most? It is a knotty problem. Among many, this hatred is the bitterer and more incurable because it is without actual cause, but is the mere effect of a difference of race, humour, and temperament. "I hate them because I hate them;" or they may say, "In no country am I so agreeably situated, no country is pleasanter to live in; but, nevertheless—I cannot help it—I hate the country and the people too."

"What a changeable, fickle, mobile race they are? they are like women and children." That is the form of reproof which is most usual towards France. But who is not fickle? In '58 divided Italy sought to remain a federation, each town wished to be independent. In '59 Italy was unitarian, crazy for unity. Grave, solemn Germany changed in one day. There were two entirely opposing Germanies before and after Sadowa: the first cursing Bismarck, the second licking his feet.

As to France, every one is so anxious to decry her

that the very persons who call her fickle are always reproaching her for not being fickle enough, of being too long-suffering under unworthy rule; they blame us for having endured our last Government for twenty years.

This is a deserved and serious blame. Yes, France has been too patient. She has given us all an unheard-of example of patience; but there were reasons for it, which may explain though not justify it, and there are extenuating circumstances. I will try to say one word about them.

France has great aspirations; she wings her flight very high, often so high that a fall is inevitable. She sees a lofty aim, but it is an aim too far removed for the path to it, or for the means to take that path, to be accessible. She fails, and is discouraged. "Quæsivit cœlo lucem, ingemuitque repertâ." The world is then pitiless. It was so to Icarus. The wretch who fails must always be stoned.

The lightning gleam of '89—that legislative formula of all the dreams which a great epoch had of Liberty—disappears for a while in the immense war made on us by Europe. The yet fairer gleam of February, '48—universal suffrage—that effort to obtain absolute justice, by which poor France appeals magnanimously to all classes to decide her fate, seems lost for ever. The world jeers; and yet the idea is a fact, and is so substantial that our enemies themselves make use of it and invoke it. Prussia has only been able to delude credulous Germany by beguiling her with an empty and hollow simulacrum of this new right, of this sure ideal of future civilization.

Let us congratulate those who have not these precocious and sublime impulses, nor these recoils and failures. An even mediocrity, often flat, and stale, and subject to the follies of the past, is at least more consistent, and as such imposes on all, and inspires esteem and respect. Absurdities are cloaked by a dignified attitude of external composure. May we be permitted to say, If you seem more logical, it is that in reality you are less so; you are not impeded like France by the difficulties caused by the search after, and the exigencies of, absolute justice. Moreover, there is this reason for the halting step of France—she is like all well-organized creatures, dual, and her parts being diverse, balance and sometimes contradict each other.

France is a nation having two orders: the peasant and the workman.

It is certain that if one of these classes disappeared by a revolution, France would be more uniform, more in harmony with herself. The world says to her often, Look at wise England—how consistent she is! With her the mechanic is dominant, the looms of Manchester prevail. The peasant has perished. Two millions of labourers (by no means peasants) who cultivate the earth weigh nothing in the balance against an industrial population of fifteen or twenty millions. God keep us from such unity! We have twenty-six millions of peasants, and ten millions of workmen. These two elements are, of course, a care to France. But then what national strength is manifested in having firmly maintained this old rural France, in which four millions of families (twenty millions of individuals) have a vested share in the property of the country. The conservatism of the peasant, the progress of the workman, cause between them an alternate advance and recoil which ends in a crisis; but the restless impatience of the workman is fastened to a strong cable, to an anchor, for the son of the soil is only too immoveable. France does not emigrate like England and Germany. All our social questions are agitated in the heart of the nation, and are illumined and corrected by experiences which are not always happy for us, but which, at least, are instructive to the world. They profit by our failures. They improve on them. They blame us, but they follow us.

It is this duality, and not an inherent love of tumults, that caused the misfortune of our fatal 2nd of December. The workmen of Paris, who often see the future more clearly than the present, insisted that the people should be the only army, and the army was composed of the peasants and sons of peasants. The sons out of revenge, the fathers evoking the legend of 1814, as to the defence of the country, exhumed between them a mythic Napoleon, and re-elected him Tyrant.

They thought (by some fetish process of thought) that it was the same Napoleon, and were, therefore, somewhat surprised at what they had done. This one, who was such a contrast in word and speech to the other, thought himself all the more bound to prove his family origin, by re-establishing militarism. And yet how changed, how diverse were the circumstances. France, laborious France, pre-occupied with her internal organization, her transits, her roads, her railways, did not dream of war.

We are always considered, be it complimentary or otherwise, as the inventors of the scourge of this century, militarism. Observe, however, that the technical war-terms, the costumes, the uniforms, are for the most part German. The type of war, in 1780, was Prussia, and the France of Louis XVI. imitated it awkwardly. Prussia, who was the first to propose the dismemberment of Poland, entered with eagerness into the idea of the dismemberment of France, and invaded it in 1792. All Europe threw itself on France as a prey. That is the origin of the wars with which we are reproached. France was peace itself in '89, but in '93 it had 749,000 men in arms. How was such an army to be fed? Having repulsed Europe, the Directory tried the dangerous experiment of discharging 300,000 men. This act ruined the Directory and created Bonaparte. The 300,000 retired soldiers acclaimed him. The 500,000 starved soldiers, who remained over and above, were fed by him in an offensive war. I recall with horror a period of which I only saw the end. France, in ten years only, 1804 to 1814, lost 1,700,000 soldiers.

That is the official figure. Shall we reproach Napoleon the First alone? No. It is but right to acknowledge that such an earthquake having commenced, or been impelled, it was not easy to stop it. War engendered war. But who commenced it? Answer ye foes, answer ye accusers, who began it? You!

Sprung from such a source, from such a tradition of blood, the Second Empire was ominous to Europe. What would it do? What was the silent one plotting? What stroke of policy would the morrow reveal? It was impossible to fathom. Neither the man himself, nor his circle of followers, were attractive or inspired confidence. And yet let us remind Europe, which condemns us for our patience, that *her* long suffering, *her* submission, *her* homage to this false phantom of war, was more admirable still. Russia, which had conquered Napoleon the Great, humbled itself to this man. All humbled themselves. At the Tuileries there was a Court composed of kings, as his uncle at his shows had had a "pit of kings" ("un parterre de rois"). Foreign nations yoked themselves to his chariot. With what delirious frenzy the Italians thronged after him at Milan! How all of these reproached us, as the irreconcilables, because we did not rally round the favourite of fortune! The proud English, how did they receive him? And, in spite of her natural shrinking, did not their Queen appear beside him at Cherbourg? He was the only monarch in Europe who seemed to sit on the throne with a solid basis. Was he not one (as it was believed) with that vast nation of labourers, who are not fickle or quick to doubt, and who lent him their formidable support?

But what did he do meanwhile for them? He was ungrateful and variable—undecided between them and the shopkeepers. This inconsistency did not justify his name of the "Rural Emperor." For more than ten years, against the farming interests of the country, he let loose the Stock Exchange speculations, created credits without funds, towards which flowed the checked capital of agriculture. Agriculture would therefore have languished had not a great industrial progress, which had been commenced for years, and which developed itself to the incalculable advantage of the new reign, enriched the whole farming portion of France. The chief work of the period—the net-work of railroads—created numberless carriage roads, and these roads were reached by millions of country by-roads. This was an Herculean effort, which occupied France twenty years.

But what one cannot lay too much stress on is this—that this work, which absorbed the peasants and farmers, and made them forgetful of their political liberties, was a great step towards social liberty. The peasant of the south and west, loaded with debt under Louis Philippe, burdened with mortgages, serf of the proprietor, or the money-lending citizen, was able, in a measure, to liberate himself,—to strike the earth on which he stood, and say, "It is mine." How was it? By a miracle—

though a simple one. Until then, the man, his land, and the fruit of his land, were prisoned and confined. They produced, but did not sell. France was a solid, inert body, without any circulation. Circulation was established. Now the produce of the south goes to the north and is sold at a great price in Paris and everywhere up to St. Petersburg. There are no more seasons now. The north eats during the spring the fruits of the summer and of the autumn.

Then came what none expected. England, rich and fond of travelling, learns to appreciate and to desire a new species of food. She leaves off her old beverage, which is so monotonous and so tasteless. She asks for, she buys, she imports our western produce. Ships are freighted with it. How many peasants, how many farmers, by that commerce alone have made their fortune.

Those who reproach the French peasant for being too easily bribed by this reward for his labour, are unfeeling. Are they ignorant of how much he has suffered for centuries—nay, until recently? The poor wretch, starving for so long, found himself, by a concourse of fortuitous circumstances, happy enough to be able to eat and thrive.

Now do you understand why the Empire lasted so long? The peasants (the great majority of the country) were not impatient to change this new state of ease, this genuine liberty, which freed them from the farmers and small landholders. They could understand

and value this liberty better than political liberty, about which they comprehended little. They were not aware that political liberty includes all others. They were ignorant of the abyss into which their faithless and unsteady guide was about to plunge them.

The mass of the nation—especially the agricultural masses—were so far from desiring war, that when the Government, confronted by the enormous armament of Germany, decreed the institution of the Garde Mobile, it could not carry out the decree. While labour-wages rose so high, the peasant could not deprive himself of his natural help, his son, to hire a labourer. Deputies were elected on their swearing to vote for peace. The prefects wrote to the Emperor that peace was the desire of the whole country. The plébiscite was obtained only by this atrocious lie. It was to ensure peace. I have before me now the engravings which were then circulated by millions. Here are two columns—the Noes, underneath which are sketches of the pillage of the reds, of the war party burning cottages and flaming harvests. And under the Yes—the amiable, smiling figure of Peace, which the Emperor guaranteed, harvests, vintages, full barns, and overflowing cellars. They voted Yes for Peace, and they obtained War.

CHAPTER IV.

THE AUTHORS OF THE WAR—GERMAN ESPIONAGE.

It has been proved, stated, acknowledged, certified—it is a fact as universally known as that the sun is in the sky—that during three or four years Prussian spies have been among us for the purpose of observing a country which had no suspicion of them—a hospitable land which received them admirably—welcomed them, and concealed nothing from them.

Who says it? The Prussians themselves.

They had already boasted, in 1866, that they had observed, studied closely, Austria, while she was their friend and ally. They arrived at Sadowa, knowing perfectly the Austrian plan of the campaign—the lists of their armies to the very last soldier. What marvellous prescience! It is clear that all these precise details had been simply purchased in the government offices at Vienna.

But their dealings with France differed widely from

this. What patient, persistent artifice; what a betrayal of confidence! What disguises which have been now revealed, acknowledged—what lies; what a frightful abuse of human speech!

It is easy to understand that these Prussian spies, these draughtsmen, photographers, engineers, &c., who came to sketch our fortresses, our mountain passes, would have only been able to send their external outlines, and would not have so thoroughly learned that which is only acquired by time—the interior of localities—if they had not cross-questioned the Germans who for so many years have been domiciled in our country. From these trustworthy sources they derived, not, as in Austria, actual military statistics and figures, but all that can be known about *such* a town, *such* a village, *such* a farm, *such* a house, confided by the host seated at the hearth to those who had dwelt with him in domestic intimacy, as familiar friends. All that could be made use of by the invaders was thus learned: they could count the grain, the cattle which their host could furnish, and could note at a glance what could be carried off.

You will exclaim and say, "What exaggeration!" No. The Prussians are proud of this, and boast of it with a cynical pride. The Germans, with their broad laugh, say, "Yes, it is all true. We were very artful, very cunning; we are a clever people." They appear in the places where they had been received and fed. "It is I!" calls out the mason from Baden; "It is I!" says the brewer of Metz, or the tailor of the Loire.

I could quote hundreds of such,—ex-intimates, ex-servants, who have returned as Uhlans.

I have read many histories, but none like this one. Never in the history of the whole world has such a thing happened, such a plan pursued for so long on such a wide scale,—one may say by a whole nation of hospitably-received travellers, and, what is worse still, by a whole people of former guests, our tradespeople, our merchants, our workmen, our servants; in short, all that tribe of persons who are usually considered as friends.

The corollary would be a sad one if we deduced it literally. Beware of being hospitable. If you see a stranger in peril or in need at your gates, you must bolt your doors and load your guns. Take care he has no arms; but if he becomes acquainted with the spot, if he notices a rickety shutter, a broken blind, he will probably return to-morrow with a host of armed companions. A wolf comes — no matter; but a man. Good heavens! a man! that is a far more ferocious animal. Woe to you, if it be a man——

It is the first explosion of indignation which thus expresses itself. But we must cast aside all the counsels of a base prudence. It is more becoming to a man who possesses a mind and a heart to examine these phenomena, and the singular, and, thank God, rare causes which have induced such a perversion of human nature.

To understand it, we must put ourselves in their

place, and try to comprehend the smoke-distorted visions which fill a German brain between his stove, his tobacco, and his beer.

"Elsewhere there is a morality; but there is no morality in France; therefore there is none to be used towards France. Against France everything is permissible."

"France is hideously corrupt. I do not know much about it, but look at French novels; and then, in '67, when I was in Paris, what a fast life I led; were not those Anonymas I amused myself with French? No matter, I have a right to say that France is corruption itself."

"She is still the revolutionary, infidel, Voltairian Sodom, that recognizes no authority and possesses no faith. She waits the scourge she has deserved; a merited chastisement dealt by God, a great expiation. That scourge I will become. Something whispers to me, 'Return. That guilty land, which is so wealthy, so fertile, which has such abundant cellars of burgundy and champagne, deserves to be *visited*.'" The *visit* of the Lord was once used as a touching pietistic phrase. It reminds me of what an English correspondent wrote last August to the English, in favour of the Germans and against France, "The Germans, as a rule, are a Christian people."

That they should have thirty systems, at least, more or less atheistic, no matter; that they should believe in nihilism, in negation of negation, never mind, the party opposed to the Pietists will say—all that is nothing. With German *gemüth*, a certain Germanism, so to speak, we have, moreover, a religious sentimentality which *is* Christian, perhaps more than Christian, which calls upon us to reform impious and corrupt France. To do that, all means are good. To spy, which in any other case would be odious, is to use an allowable weapon here. A thinker observes, a patriot observes, the enemy. He is yet our friend, but to-morrow he may be our enemy!

Observe! It was very easy to observe France. France is open. There are no gates here. All strangers enter it at once. That which costs money elsewhere, in the schools and museums, with us is gratis. We suffer from this, but we persist in it. We educated the clever man who stopped us so long before Sebastopol. We educate our enemies.

In all places of trust the Germans are more favourably received by us than any other strangers. Their application, their persistency, make them preferable to persons of even greater ability. Their scientific attainments enable them to reach the highest professorships. The Institute has received them with solid titles of honour: M. Hase and M. Mohl have very justly and fairly become French.

In all inferior arts and trades, what a crowd of Germans.* Tailors and boot-makers are often real

* The expulsion of the German workmen was unnecessary in certain provinces in which they could not act as spies, and

artists, who make an attentive study of the human form, and evince great facility in making their art adapt itself to its irregularities, and in even rectifying them. The best of these are often Germans.

Many persons now-a-days seek as nurses and nursery-maids German women, to teach German to their children. Even when there are no children in the family, they are preferred for another reason. What can be more gentle than a German woman? She has milk, instead of blood, in her veins. She seems born to obey; and, as a lady said once to me, speaking of her German *bonne*, "her docility seems personal devotion and tenderness. If you give orders to an English girl, she has certain little obstinate notions in her small head, this or that, which she considers a dogma or a principle, and it is a question if she obeys you; but if I tell my German what to do or leave undone, everything melts into its place, all is honey and oil, beyond even what I could anticipate. Every time I return home from a walk or a visit, I can scarcely prevent the poor devoted creature from kneeling down to take off my shoes. She used to say she would never leave me; but, after all, one fine morning she disappeared, and I find her now engaged in a family

they were regretted there. In the Eure et Loir, one of my female relatives has often interfered on behalf of their families who had been expelled also. Her husband employed 590 Germans and Prussians in his manufactory, and would have willingly kept them.

who are no friends of mine. Still, one likes German servants better than all others. I do not know why."

It is easy to explain. German men and women have, besides, a natural docility of character, another quality which is inherent in their race—a respect for, or instinctive worship of, authority, no matter of what kind. Manners, which in other races would seem servile and would repel us, only make us smile, and are by no means displeasing in the Germans; they are so impregnated with a sentiment which appears almost filial. This enables them to endure harsh words and even ill-treatment from their superiors, the bullying of their officers, and a military discipline which would degrade any other race.

The idea of class among the Celts is, that the chief is merely a relative. In the ancient Germanic tribes the chief is a father, and possibly a severe one. That patriarchal notion subsists even now. The Emperor Francis, that old bigot, who was so ruthless to his captives at Spielberg, was not less to the people he received every week, "our good Franz." The curious fact is, that the representatives of the Imperial authority, down to its very lowest degree, successfully appealed to this popular sentiment. "In the name of the good Franz," they extorted from the peasants, the soldiers, the ignorant, the details which were useful to their police. "What, would you not have confidence in your father the Emperor, and in us, who speak to you in his name?"

When Madame Teleki, one of the Hungarian martyrs, was imprisoned for so many years with her devoted friend, Madlle. Clara Loveï, at the castle of Küsstein, the Italian and Hungarian soldiers who had them in custody were so touched by their misfortunes, that they served them with the utmost zeal, carrying their letters, performing their errands, at the peril of their lives, without revealing anything to their officers. When one regiment left, they bequeathed their tender duty to their successors. In spite of the rigorous surveillance of the Austrian officers, they could not extort a syllable from them. Would such fidelity have been found in Germans? Would it not have been imposed on them as a duty, to *observe* the prisoners who were the enemies of their father-emperor? This infantine obedience, this absolute faithfulness even in indelicate requirements, is a barbaric virtue. We understand it, as we understand the coarse goodfellowship which in certain parts of the south draws together the officer and the soldier. But how does it exist in the north, where authority assumes so haughty and arid an aspect; where it proceeds from a pride both of caste and rank, and is represented by that poor, half-ruined gentry, of an incredible insolence naturally, and whom a military education of the most pedantic kind has rendered ruder and harder than the Russians themselves? A soldier thus drilled, can he maintain, under such severe discipline, that old German sentiment of allegiance which preserved him from becoming degraded? He

3

will be brave before the enemy, doubtless; but he will not be brave before his chief if he chooses to exact from him things which are scarcely military, such as police duties and others, which would be equally dishonourable to a soldier.

Gill, one of our cleverest caricaturists, was very far from the truth when, in August, 1870, he drew the spy as a hideous mendicant or loathsome Jew, whose scared and hypocritical mien seemed to say, "Arrest me! hang me! I am a spy!"

A spy is far oftener a blonde youth with rosy cheeks and an innocent voice, who comes from the University quite fresh with his pockets full of letters of recommendation. An eminent writer said to me many years ago, "You see that cherub who has just left me, who has noted so well my lodging, and has showed me such respect: he has made me speak on a subject which is both delicate and dangerous. You will see he is going to attack me in an article in the *Gazette d'Augsbourg*." That was twenty-six years ago. Now if the young man *observes*, it is less for his newspaper than for the military police.

What a surprise it would be for Fichte, for Jalm, for the patriots of 1813, if they could see that the student they had so austerely educated had been refined, civilized, and (by means of at least three metaphysical systems) passed through the dialectic sieve of doubt and irony, until he had learned to concentrate all his philosophy into this cynical phrase of Goethe's: "I have always found it served me well to be the friend of tyrants."

I could wish I had the time to write the Sentimental Journey across France made, I suppose, in 1867, by some young *observer*, spy, philosopher, poet, writing his letters every evening, sometimes to his betrothed, sometimes to M. de Moltke. A student of books and scholastic rule, how little he will understand a country of infinite spontaneity, lights and shades, and of which the best part cannot be described. What mistakes, what follies he posts off! But the figures extracted for the staff will have their use. He will point out the resources the invasion will find in each town, in each house, in the very house he has just come from. Who could distrust him! He looks as innocent as the girl he accompanies on the piano. The more timid, the more awkward he is, the more he will inspire confidence, the more he will be able to betray.

And how easily spies can now circulate! The suppression of passports, the world-wide *incognito*, the confused throng of the crowds at the railroads, everything helps and favours the iniquitous system.

As a tourist or as a tradesman, he could see, he could mark everything. Engineers dressed in blouses, and who looked like peasants, made drawings and photographs of the passes of the Vosges and of our fortifications. In one of the mines of the Eastern provinces many Prussians engaged themselves as miners, and during many months could study all the environs—describe them at their leisure. Sometimes they acted strange little dramas, with which they beguiled confidence. Two persons had left Montpellier and wished to return to Paris (an eminent surgeon and M. Daly, the well-known architect), and had found, with a great deal of difficulty, a coachman at Chartres, who promised to attempt to get them through. These gentlemen, as they set off, were followed by a respectable-looking man, plunged in grief, who entreated them to permit him to accompany them. He was a merchant of Paris, settled at Bucharest, anxiously expected in Paris by his family, his wife, and his little children. They allowed him to share the carriage, and talked openly before him. At ten leagues from Paris they halted for awhile, and, missing him for a moment, came up to him as he was explaining, in good German, all about them to a Prussian officer. They were obliged to turn back and return to Montpellier.

But the travelling spy could not have gathered together so much minute and precise information if he had not been aided by the spy in the household, who naturally is acquainted far more thoroughly with everything. Therefore, to obtain complaisant answers to his questions, the former, you may be sure, addresses himself to his own countrymen, to the Germans domiciled in the place, and at the beershop where one goes to drink, and which has for its customers the best families in the town. The tailor, seated cross-legged on his table, is only too happy to chatter and reply to questions. The gossips of the neighbourhood usually gather round him, he knows the slightest detail, and can speak of numberless little peculiarities which reveal the whole district. The officers who came later to make requisitions, had no need to see the lists of contributors or of tax-payers. They knew perfectly well what each village could pay.

People were surprised that at Ablon, on the Seine, it was known that a certain farm had twenty-five cows, instead of twenty. But they would have been still more surprised if it could be published, how much these invaders knew of internal, domestic, and apparently useless details. Their insatiable curiosity was also amply, and, without much effort, satisfied by our German servants; the good creatures are only too glad to talk to an honest compatriot. If he is young their confidence is simply limitless. It was a very clever trick of the Prussians in the last century to make use of their handsomest men to flirt with the favourite maids of their great Viennese ladies. Fauche Borel, the celebrated spy of Prussian Neufchatel, was as fair as a girl, and his beautiful face gave him access everywhere.

A German of great good sense, who has looked at these events from a high point of view, has said, "You must not say *Væ victis!* but *Væ victoribus!* The defeated is only ruined. The victor is degraded."

If this state of things were to become permanent, it would be necessary to erect a tomb, a sepulchral monument, to the antique German virtues now buried. The hero now is not Roland, but the man who betrayed him, Ganelon de Mayence. The hero is no longer Siegfried, but the traitor Hagen.

Sleep, Honour, sleep, Good-faith, beneath this tomb; sleep, plighted word, truthfulness, noble simplicity, who have charmed us so long!

CHAPTER V.

ENGINES OF WAR.

The valour of Cortes, who all but singly undertook the conquest of an empire of a million of men, is a celebrated fact. But we cannot deny that his weapon had a great deal to do with his victories. It was the *musket* which won them.

So let us not deny the merit of the Prussians, who risked their lives in invading France with their million of men, and the strategy of whose captains is as praiseworthy as their courage. But it is certain that their weapon, the field cannon of long range, has had its share in their victories.

Their bulletins rarely fail in telling us that they owe their successes especially to their "admirable artillery." But they do not always acknowledge that in the decisive moments of an engagement, at Sedan for instance, their range was so great, that our guns could not even reach them. There was, therefore, no struggle, consequently no victory. Men were superfluous, the cannon did it all. There was no defence possible. Who were the

Germans engaged at Sedan? The Bavarian Landwehr for the most part. Their loss was not heavy. They were safely sheltered behind that circle of a thousand cannons, into the midst of which our armies were driven and crushed.

"Our soldiers," says a reliable witness, "were fire-bound within a certain distance. They, the Germans, shot at ranges of five hundred or a thousand mètres further than the French. We could fire tremendous volleys, but we had not the comfort of even hitting them. I could see them with my glasses, quietly making their coffee or boiling their soup behind their batteries." This is entirely confirmed by the Prussians themselves, who were proud of their success and of the art and calculation which had given it them. They boasted of these far more than of their gallantry and courage.

They said often, "We do not require even to see your soldiers' faces, but we know we must inevitably defeat them." Sometimes they added exultingly, "It is all settled: it will be over by Christmas or the New Year. It is a mathematical certainty." The surprise of Sadowa, where the solid army of Austria and the brave Hungarians were bewildered, thunderstruck, by a new weapon, ought to have been a sufficient warning. It was easy to guess what rapid progress would be made in the years which followed Sadowa—that after the improvement in guns, cannon would be remodelled. Machinery progresses continually. It does not advance by a sudden leap of miraculous genius, but by the gradual and successive perfecting of parts: each step onwards, however slight, leads to another, and so on. We see this in industrial—a far more complicated affair than military—machinery.

The progress of machinery is the characteristic of the age. It is a great power, peculiar to modern times, and pregnant with awful possibilities for good or for evil. The last century, in stimulating individual dexterity, has educated the workman. This century has created the iron workman and the iron soldier—in short, machinery. During the first fifty years, machinery devoted itself to the arts of peace. For the last thirty years it has served war, and has transformed it. The various arts which were combined in machinery have been more and more applied to purposes of destruction.

The history of machinery is curious and suggestive. How recent it all is. Watt died, it seems, but yesterday. Between 1776 and 1840, the scope of machinery was a benevolent one. The factories manufactured cloths and tissues, which clothed, adorned, and warmed all mankind—civilized beings as well as savages. Its forges provided at the cheapest rate the tools which are the necessary implements of art. Aided by steam, it accelerates and multiplies locomotion a hundred-fold. We poor loiterers, who hitherto had crawled on the earth and on the capricious wave, have now sure and speedy wings. We can now say with certainty, "We shall arrive on such a day, at such a minute." What thanksgivings have been sung in honour of this blessing!

But is this all? Alas! this great, imperturbable and ruthless force will lead to other results. Children and ignorant people are afraid of them. Are they wrong? Is not their antipathy prescience? Sixty years ago my parents took me to see the steam-pump at Chaillot, and the great Museum of machines at Rue St. Martin. I was stunned, overwhelmed at the giant enigma of these new forces, of these metallic workmen, of these impersonal persons, of these brass and steel hands. The Chaillot machine was as yet imperfect and rude; but as its revolutions made the walls shake, it seemed rather the foe than the servant of man. Its use was proudly pointed out to me. But I felt an instinct, rooted deep within me, which obstinately whispered what strange fatalities might exist in these unknown agents. These creatures, developed and begetting like by a mathematical progression, which was inevitable, might they not in the long run, after having gone through a phase of production, enter another of destruction? Might they not themselves destroy, or become instruments of extermination?

In the engines of war, there is the same murderous progress. One form of gun supplants another. Delvigne was destroyed by Dreysse. Dreysse was shot down by Chassepot. The same with cannon. The incomparable Paixhans was dismounted by Armstrong. Armstrong by Krupp, the hero of 1870.

The double-barrelled pistols, early invented by France, the American revolver, are the parents of an infinite number of similar weapons. A friend of mine from Geneva, saw in 1839, in the arsenal of Strasbourg, the type of a breech-loader which fired eight rounds a minute, and which in '66 was to triumph at Sadowa. Our African army had rejected it as too cumbersome. The indubitable "marvels" of the chassepot had not dazzled us. All sensible persons knew that the perfection of the gun as a weapon, would be useless (especially in the great plains of the North) before a perfected artillery at long range, which would not permit guns to approach.

The monstrous Krupp cannon, which was exhibited in Paris in 1867, was grotesque from its ponderous massiveness, and appeared to be useless except as a bastion or rampart defence. We were ignorant of the enormous manufacture of cannons of the same kind, only light and moveable ones, which went on at Magdeburg and all Prussian arsenals. The "mitrailleuse," which was the Emperor's favourite invention and hobby, which he never exhibited, but covered up with a kind of jealous mystery, was known universally in Prussia, manufactured, multiplied, but as a second-rate field-piece which could not act everywhere, and which could be rendered useless by long-range cannons.

Inventions which are conveyed from one country to another, and of which it is impossible to keep the monopoly or the secret, yet inspire a confidence and a pride in men which is quite unreasonable. We imagine too credulously that it is a new limb we acquire, an arm, a hand, a hundred hands, that it makes us equal to Briareus. A wealthy ingenious people, who up to a certain time have been ignorant of some machine or other, once put on the track soon learn to imitate it, often to surpass it, or to invent a superior one. This kind of improvisation took place at Paris and on the Loire. Light cannons were cast instantly, and Paris was soon armed with a formidable artillery.

Who shall prevent barbarians from using machinery? She is the offspring of civilization, but may turn against it and rend it. The Russians, through America, through England itself, will obtain the same powerful artillery of which the Prussians are so proud, and which I hear is already surpassed in America, both as to length of range and lightness. Arrived at this point the mechanism of Death might meet a rival yet more murderous and fulminating. Chemistry, which is seeking to develop itself on that side, will have its turn. What a horrible struggle of sciences and arts for the service of Death!

A thoughtful friend of mine was saying, "But after all these victories of machinery, which apparently are the triumphs of brute force, are actually the result of thought, invention, intellect; they are therefore the result of progress." Agreed; but this new art of killing a people at 5,000 mètres' range, without any personal risk, without being even aware of the terrible consequences of the fire; does it not involve an impassiveness, a ruthlessness, which could not belong to former wars? It is, to say the least of it, cold-blooded murder. That which was formerly the atoning grace of war, and ennobled it, was the equal peril, the self-devotion, the spirit of self-sacrifice. Men are now so wise, they calculate to such a nicety the power of matter, and trust so little to their own strength, that they all but omit it in their summing up of chances. Will they not, therefore, eventually fail in heart and spirit? The mechanician will be all; the hero nought.

When Frenchmen opposed bayonets to powder—bayonets which bring foes face to face, dazzle the eyes and chill the nerves—they were courageous, and acted as brave men. "We shall see," they exclaimed, "who stands calm and firm before the flash of steel." They would have felt disgraced to attack an enemy, as is done now, after having battered him with a storm of shells.

When Gustavus Adolphus, with 30,000 Swedes, fell on Germany, and threw such dismay on the great armies of Europe, he employed no machinery. He even put aside the heavy arms, the ponderous iron corslets, which were then used. He wore but his buff jacket. He perished, but what matter, he won. He made the cause of liberty triumph, and through his heroism the Treaty of Westphalia was imposed on his enemies.

CHAPTER VI.

CORRUPTION OF THE EMPIRE.

Prussia must first thank her weapons, secondly, the perfect knowledge she had obtained (most unscrupulously) of the country; but most of all she ought to be grateful to the French administration, to our military commissariat, which yielded up our army to our enemies, starved and defeated, beforehand.

We gave Germany the respite of fifteen days, which were necessary to her, to mobilise her troops. And in spite of that delay all preparation on our part was omitted. It is a known fact, that at Wörth, the cuirassiers who made that famous charge, at the close, had not eaten for thirty hours. It is stated that at Sedan our army, which was being thrust forward from Châlons by forced marches, had only provided one small piece of bread a day for each soldier.

This is not wonderful when one considers the corruption of the Imperial Government. It was rottenness itself.

It sprang from gamblers and adventurers—Morny, Magnan, &c. But the further back we go, all the Bonapartist party (that long conspiracy) had but one wisdom—chance; one fixed idea—their star.

Louis Napoleon was born, so to speak, in a lottery-office, nursed on the knees of Josephine, his Creole grandmother, who, with her coloured servant and Madame Lenormant, was always having her fortune told, and consulting the cards which were to reveal her destiny. It is well known that when she married the great warrior she gave him a black ring, on which was engraved on one side, "To Destiny." Beneath were characters which time only revealed. (Waterloo.)

Belief in the improbable, the absurd, the miraculous, and the contempt of all right reason, were but the natural results of the reign of Napoleon the Great. It was forgotten that the most fabulous absurdity and folly were scarcely to be counted such by one who had received from the Revolution its enchanted, infallible, weapon. I mean that prodigious army which could commit faults because it knew how to repair them, by sheer force of courage and fire of blood. Women were infatuated about that army; Queen Hortense found in it her chief agents.

Josephine's fetish belief in fate, in chance, in her star, with the false notion that the Napoleons possessed or inherited some right bestowed originally by the people, were the religion of the party.

The hero who was being nurtured for these high

destinies, and who, it was whispered, was the son of Napoleon, was the eldest and most manly of Hortense's sons. Louis was a fair, dreamy, lymphatic youth, obedient and quiet, and who, under his preceptor's care, the erudite Le Bas, would have been a scholar or at least an archæologist. To have written "Cæsar" would have been the task of his whole life; but the brother died, and it was necessary to make Louis a hero. He was well drilled in all bodily exercises, but he could not be made into a soldier.

He was like a racquet-ball under the hand of his party. He was sent on at Strasbourg and Boulogne; he risked nothing in the mad enterprises into which he was thrown by the giddy and needy fools, who staked on him their chances and their hopes, because he was bucklered by the name of Napoleon. He was born to be imprisoned, and he was resigned to it. He was more at leisure there for his chosen studies. He had a somnambulistic look, which made one think that in that pent-up life, where waking and sleeping are blended in one, he indulged in the enervating dreams produced by opium.

He was so habitually mute that people could interpret him as they chose. His silence was a weapon. In '48 he succeeded because he never spoke. The gamblers, the desperadoes, who were his companions, risked everything, and had audacity for him and for themselves. We are assured that he hesitated on the 2nd December, and did not desire the massacre. In a cautious note, now published for the first time, he throws the blame on Morny, who had changed his orders, and added the words "Shoot them."

Such an act, however, which roüsed the indignation of the whole world, caused him to be surrounded by the gang who had perpetrated it. These were men of a merely subordinate kind for the most part, by no means prepared for the *rôle* which they were about to play. It is certain that St. Arnaud, when entrusted with the great task of the Crimean war, had no idea of the geography of those countries, but sent for some maps from the shops in the Quai Voltaire. He was entirely ignorant that in our War Office we had the best drawn maps in the world.

In '59, when we went to Italy, we had never studied the country which we went to free, while the Austrians knew it by heart. The *Moniteur* makes the following confession four times, "We have been surprised." MacMahon at Magenta, Niel at Solferino, saved, it is said, the Emperor. The army saved itself, the soldiers repaired the faults and the astonishing carelessness of their generals.

The Emperor has a quality which is equally dangerous in war as in politics. He advances boldly, becomes alarmed, and retreats. This accounts for so many miscarriages. The affair of the Crimea had in it a certain grandeur; but he could not carry it out to the end by rousing Poland. To liberate Italy was well; but to be complete, he should have stirred up Hungary.

4

Between Kossuth and Austria he leaned towards Austria. As to Italy, he did not desire Italy to be strong; he wished it to be divided; and he gained the implacable hatred of the Italians, whom he came to save.

His own indecision, his own fear of the Revolution, might have made him commit these faults; but his fatal surroundings—the influence of his brother at the beginning, of his wife at the end, of his career—weighed unworthily on him. Without the first he had not probably persisted in his murderous deportations; without the second he would not have thwarted and finally alienated Italy for the sake of the Pope, and the folly of the Mexican enterprise would never have taken place.

His own opinions are vague and fickle. While he granted M. Duruy a revolutionary power, which might have ruined our aristocratic colleges, and made each student a workman, he made our military schools essentially aristocratic and clerical; the officers were chosen only among the well-born, the rich, or the sons of the high officials, who had been educated by Jesuits and friars for the Polytechnic schools, for Saint Cyr, &c. France, under this Spanish and priestly influence, would have lost that which has been the making of our glorious armies—the principle of equality; the soldier would have been discouraged, the subaltern would have been arrested in his career, there would have arisen that Junkerism which makes Prussia so odious and so intolerable to Germany.

But what a light suddenly flashed on him at the close of his reign, and how startlingly both the system and the man were revealed.

There never was such a sudden shock as that of 1869; the Emperor was worse than dethroned, he was branded, pilloried.

The indignation felt by France at having slept so profoundly and so long, at having ignored so much and borne so much, made the awakening an implacable Nemesis. He was literally anatomised, not by the scalpel, but by a piercing light which revealed the inward man entirely—entrails, nerves, all. No man has ever been subject to such minute exploring of his whole being.

The secret-service money, the bribes, the affairs of Morny, had very much degraded the empire. Mexico, which was nothing but a swindle, had been revealed in '67, by the abrupt scene at St. Cloud, when the furious and insane Charlotte told the Emperor and the Empress the same terrible truths which posterity will utter. Maximilian was abandoned and perished. And as one ghost recalls the memory of other ghosts, all those of the 2nd December reappeared, evoked by the book of Ténot. What availed it to deny them? The authority of the *Moniteur* itself triumphantly sums up the murders and massacres of the period, and draws up the indictment for them. All those pale witnesses arise in their shrouds, and defiling silently by, point out the pages where the murderers accuse themselves and mark themselves out for eternal condemnation. All shuddered who saw, but only one spoke. An heroic *gamin*, who was careless of the enormous power which crushed us, broke the spell. Nothing can be more characteristic of France. Let historians remember that in June, 1869, a youth, then but little known, did that which no one dared to do in Europe. All the monarchs of Europe were bowing to the man at the Tuileries, and styling themselves his cousins and brothers. They revered in him the master of an army of 500,000 men. But this youth laughs at him. As power against power he declares war, and signs his name Rochefort.

From thence proceeded an entire literature. The mourning of these late months cannot make one forget the brilliant escapades of the *Rappel*, and so many of the provincial journals, full of wit, fire, and anger. We old men gave welcome to this gay outburst of youth. "Are there still young men? Are there still talents and promise in France? Does France yet exist?" The patience of the Imperial spectre was both surprising and alarming. He remembered that his silence had succeeded in '49. To let this eruption, this fire of straw, go out, was the plan. Meanwhile he called up a mask to act a vain comedy of parliamentary institutions. It was the best mask he could select; for the masker was genuine, and believed in himself. His name was Olivier.

That Napoleon should change his nature,—that he should forswear the Napoleonic legend of blood and roguery,—that the wolf should become a dog, a good shepherd's dog, who could hope it? One morning he takes off his dog's skin, and reappears as himself. He calls to his peasants, to the great, credulous, uneducated country which he had already deceived. Everything was changed. Light was dawning. To obscure all things, to steal the voice of the people, nothing was spared. It was an enormous crime. Official manifestoes, programmes, journals, the horrible engravings I have mentioned, to alarm the rural masses, to brutalise them, audaciously marked out the Reds and appealed to a social conflict. The Reds, it was said, are precipitating France towards war, towards perdition. The Reds burned the farms, the people were told, and paid those they hired to do so 600 francs, so one of my friends was told not far from Cherbourg. The accidental rick-burnings which often follow a great drought were thus explained; and my young friend, the son of Dr. Bertillon, narrowly escaped death for arson. Since, in the Dordogne, the peasants have burned alive a man who was considered a Red.

It is curious to reflect how large a portion lies have had in the events of this wonderful year 1870.

In France and in Germany two panics have swept everything before them. Panics artfully arranged and kindled.

In France the boldest possible lie deceived the country. It voted, appalled by the fear of war, anarchy, fire; and strong through this vote for Peace, our Sovereign declared War.

On the other hand, how did M. de Bismarck carry off Germany—those kingdoms, so lately reunited, yet so agitated; the South, so uncertain, so reluctant? How did he seduce a mass of a million of men,—a number which has never been gathered together since the Crusades, the old barbaric invasions. By fear, by a well-considered and scenic panic, a phantasmagoria, which shocked and drew them on at once. "Here they come, the Algerians, the Zouaves, the Turcos! Save your wives, your children!"

Bavaria paused. They were told a falsehood—"The French have passed the Rhine!"

Here was a surprise on both sides. Bismarck had been preparing his for three years; for he felt that without war and its maddening fever he could never muzzle Germany. By the war he escaped the ultimate resistance, the dying breath of German liberty.

The Emperor thought he had no shelter but war against the awful uprising of French liberty, and its revenge. Paris terrified him; and when he was in the arms of his good brother King William, he said (very aptly, it must be confessed), "We have both the same enemy."

CHAPTER VII.

THE EMPEROR AND SEDAN.

Is Louis Napoleon a Frenchman? What is his country? His native language is German. He spoke it in Switzerland and in the college at Augsbourg. His government was a foreign government presided over by a German and a Spaniard. A thousand petty details could prove how ignorant he was of France, and how impossible it was for him to be acquainted with her, not having the innate tact or the wit peculiar to our nation.

His proclamation after Wörth (a first defeat, and certainly therefore not of paramount importance,) caused every one to exclaim: "He is no Frenchman!" A Frenchman might have anticipated evil, but he would have had too much cleverness and too much presence of mind to betray it so thoroughly.

He heard of that defeat the next day fortuitously (what an administration!) by a photographer and two escaped newspaper writers, and he lost his head so completely, that with such large forces still left, he had not the forethought to defend the defiles of the Vosges. They were left so defenceless that the Prussians would not believe it possible, and were afraid at first of entering them. They feared some snare or stratagem. In that first desperate proclamation the Emperor called on all for aid.

"On all! All meant France." And he was more afraid of France than of anything else.

He called to arms, and yet he refused arms. He did not even arm Alsace, which was in such danger. He gave them out some old useless firelocks. There were abundant chassepots in our arsenals, but they were incomplete; and for fear of the people getting hold of them, one essential portion of the weapon was deficient in each.

The Emperor, the man of the people, for whom the people had voted, feels himself insecure in that direction, and will be saved by the army alone. The army has been cut in two and is shut up in Metz. To attempt to relieve it with too small a body of troops is to perish. MacMahon, a true soldier, feels this. He knows that the only chance of safety is in retreat towards Paris, giving the new army that support and confidence which the vast resources of such a city could command. He was overruled by Palikao. I am not an historian here. Others may follow day by day, step by step, this prodigious and terrible drama.

At Metz, Bazaine, who might still with his 150,000 men have cut his way out, so says Changarnier, allowed himself to be permanently surrounded, hoping (was it through the messages of Bismarck? or of the Emperor?) that, with his excellent army, he would be the arbiter, the mediator of the situation.

The letters of General Wimpffen, 11th and 19th September, and letters from many other officers, have firmly established as a fact, that the Emperor refused every offer which was made to cut a way through the Prussians. It is true that the murderous artillery I have before mentioned surrounded the army from the heights. But would the troops which occupied them have resisted a final, desperate, and furious attack? would they have stood by their guns? Very reliable witnesses — Swiss, surgeons, Geneva-cross-men from both camps—assure us that the majority of these troops were the Bavarian landwehr.

The Emperor forgot he was no longer the commander-in-chief, and hoisted the white flag without the knowledge of Wimpffen. He sent one of his household to the King of Prussia.

The infamy was accomplished. The surrender was without conditions.

But that which has most improved the cause of the victors is, that according to the testimony of the Swiss who were there, no one dared to tell our soldiers what had befallen them. They feared the frenzy of their despair. I read in the *Journal of Geneva* (not friendly to the French) a letter from its correspondent, 8th October: "This is what I have been told, not by ten or fifteen, but by more than two hundred prisoners, in different hospitals and barracks, where there could have been no possibility of collusion between them. 'We were only told to lay down our arms, and that we could go away. A squadron accompanied us to the gate of Sedan, and instead of our being allowed to go free, we were driven into a kind of marshy island.' . . . There they were left to starve for several days."

The King of Prussia became quite softened to the Emperor. He had rendered him a great service, he spoke German, and more than all, kings make common cause together. He felt that the Emperor was quite sincere when he said, "We have the same enemy."

"But this war?"

"It was France, not I, who wished it."

If ever a falsehood was uttered it was this.

It was a solemn and a memorable scene. It recalls that in the beginning of Genesis; where Adam in his cowardly terror stammers forth, "The woman gave unto me, and I did eat."

CHAPTER VIII.

THE UNCONQUERED SPIRIT OF FRANCE.

It is strange that great nations should ignore each other so absolutely as they do. Humanitarians are fools to believe that the walls, hedges, barriers, which were between them of old, are done away with. On the contrary, a few antiquated prejudices may have died out; but a growing personality separates more and more nations and individuals.

The Germans, for instance, since Sadowa, for three years and more, have, with an earnest, attentive, methodical study, *observed* France. Every optical aid has been employed. Using the magnifying-glasses given by passion, hatred, envy, and fanaticism, the young devout missionaries of Teutonic mania came among us, to examine everything and send home accurate statistics about everything. These military and other details, concentrated under the strong glasses of the old strategist who inspires the whole machinery of war with his steel nerves and iron soul, resulted in combinations, which formed a new astrology. He could calculate it all, like a problem in mathematics, and marked with his strong finger on the calendar of 1870 the day of the death of France !

The solution was erroneous. France still lives !

Vanity of science ! emptiness of human knowledge ! Germany, with its *Gemüth,* its great moral pretensions, knew nothing, calculated nothing but mechanical forces. Oh, land of ideality, thou didst ignore the soul !

The men of erudition, the learned antiquarians, the philologists, had said to Germany, that Alsace and Lorraine would hasten to meet their brethren—the men in the long black vests of the time of Charlemagne, the women in their red dresses, singing the old German *lieds ;* that no defence would be made, the only difficulty would be to check the Teutonic enthusiasm. They might in their new loyalty suffocate their beloved monarch ! Beyond the frontier there would be less resistance still. It was well known and noticed at the suppers of '67, during the Great Exhibition, that France was corrupt to the core, in a state of flagrant decomposition. The only dangers (beware, young men !) are those enormous cellars of champagne, where you might be overcome by those heady wines. The sixty leagues of vines which, on the hill-sides of Burgundy, upreared on their poles, look like the files of an army, may also be dangerous to you, and cause you shipwreck ; but that is all.

These ideas were naturally confirmed when Germany found in the Emperor a man educated in Germany, and who fraternised with her, and yielded up his armies to her. But it was not over. France had lost her armies, her cannons; but she had her two arms, her breast, and the fire of her heart, with which to confront the enemy.

That people who were so corrupt, it was said, and also so enervated, and apparently in a state of dissolution, are here before us, actually standing upright, opposing us. Is it possible? What a surprise! Do you think Germany will own she was mistaken? By no means. No; she shakes her head, and says piously, "How sad it is when a sinner will not submit to his punishment, or thank the rod, but struggles, and rages, and rejects all expiation! It is necessary, therefore, to increase the castigation and not to spare the Bismarck prescription—steel and fire!" Steel! Yes, steel is the thing! What a powerful stimulant to feel in one's flesh so many cruel spurs! Acupuncture is an efficacious though cruel remedy for all inertia and languor of organisation! Thanks, executioners!

What virtues have been wakened! How the fire has purified, exalted, ennobled men's souls! Let us open the Golden Legend, and write in it the names of the Government of the National Defence. Has it not been admirably loyal, faithful, true? What obliged some of its members—aged, wealthy, already rich in all the glories of talent—to accept the immense responsibilities and risk the fatal ingratitude usually experienced by the saviours of a people?

What is most striking in this Government of Paris is, not only its calm courage, but its gentleness, its humanity, its loyal modesty, and, may I say it, its youthful sincerity. Do not smile at my words. The memorable interview between Jules Favre and Bismarck will live for ever. It is folly to think that the first, because he was agitated, was the least clever of the two. His warm heart, his patriotic tears, drew from the other that acknowledgment which is his condemnation—1st, that he expects no voluntary submission from Alsace and Lorraine, that he intends to use force and make them German in spite of themselves; 2nd, that between France and Germany there will exist henceforth eternal hatred, and that he acts in that sense.

But then two Provinces are not sufficient. From the Rhine to the Alps and the Pyrenees one must have a cleaver to hack—to chop France—that we may sell and distribute our booty, and make Europe partake of it. Open the Bismarck shop—a bloody shambles—where he can say to the nations, "Who wishes to devour France?"

No, that conversation was an instructive one, and the cleverer of the two was the one who wept.

This dismemberment, this portioning off, is the true Prussian method, so ably carried out in Poland. By it Prussia is linked for ever to Russia against Germany itself. M. de Bismarck's face is that of a Russian general, and I have not deceived myself in thinking so.

The investment of Paris, which took place the 19th of September, had a strange effect on Europe. So much warmth and light emanate from Paris, that there was less light, less animation, fewer echoes in the world. It is a sublime but odious struggle. Here again the duel is between machinery and man. Our enemies do not deny that their principal force is in their artillery, and it is with that iron ring that they have girt us round.

Their great hope was in our dissensions—our interior divisions. But there were none. All were agreed. None were discordant, but some were impatient. They were heroes, who wished to rush on the enemy. They did not understand the great and arduous necessity for disciplining, forming, drilling those brave but confused masses of men, who would have perished at the first blow from their blind zeal, their headlong valour.

On looking the other day at a plan of this heroic city, bound with its red girdle of flaming forts, I saw in my mind's eye the black swarms of beings, who, on all sides, like ants, were piling up at a distance mountains upon mountains of earth, to surround and overwhelm it. I was reminded of Roland the Brave, whom Ganelon de Mayence took care, not to attack singly as man to man, but who was betrayed into an amphitheatre of rocks, in the Pyrenees, where he found himself in the midst of menacing heights. From these heights rocks could be hurled down on him. With his flashing sword he clove first one mount, then two more, as one may still see. Then he blew his magic horn and called for aid. He perished, but who dares confess he slew him. His own mighty effort destroyed him. His passionate appeal for help to the nations—deaf then, alas ! as they are now.

CHAPTER IX.

VANDALISM.

A SENSIBLE German lady said to me, "I would have given my life so that the war had ended at Sedan."

She was right. German honour was then safe. All wrong was veneered over by the deceptive glosses employed by Bismarck. "The French began, the Germans are victorious, and have taken no undue advantage of their victory." Europe would have been deceived. Englishmen, who lived in the camp and at the table of Bismarck, guaranteed German gentleness, moderation, prudence. An English nobleman, at the commencement of the war, writes like a simpleton. "Rob? Why, they would not take a pin."

But the sad reality has now been displayed—an undercurrent of brutality and of unexpected barbarism. Moreover, they have evinced a cynical surprise, which is a disgrace to them—a surprise that any one should resist them. Brave men appreciate brave men, and honour the indomitable valour of an enemy. Let me mention here an anecdote told me by some Hungarians: "In

'98, the Hungarian cavalry had decimated ours, but finally ours retrieved themselves, and drove the others before them to the edge of a precipice. But they would not surrender, and were falling into the abyss. The French, full of generous admiration at such valour, called out, 'Cease firing.'"

Besides the prodigious respect which Germans feel for force, their worship of authority makes them pitiless towards the valour which resists Might, consecrated by Success, and which does not acknowledge the judgment of God. "What! dare resist all these Kings—these Highnesses in person, who are doing them the honour to sack and bombard their towns? What audacity! what blasphemy! Yes; they are the true sons of iniquity and of anarchy, that accursed race, born of the teeth of the revolutionary dragon! If God's thunder does not crush them, let the cannons of our kings annihilate them."

"It has been a very great surprise to us," said a judicious young man, a cool and impartial spectator, a Swiss surgeon; "we have always thought, considering their famous universities, their learned men, their literature, that the Germans were superior to us in everything."

One thing is indubitable now, and which hitherto we were all unconscious of, that this great nation, placed so loftily in certain respects, is inferior to other nations, in the low vulgarity of certain classes, and yet more so, in these bastard branches of her nationality, which Germany projects out of herself; in her far-off emigrations, where the best part of a nation becomes effaced, and even more in those nearer countries which she utilises by a covetous trade, or over which she tyrannises through her officials, stewards, clerks, &c.—I speak of Russia.

Our southern peasants and the Italians are, in the very lowest classes, courteous and polite. They might pass for disguised gentlemen. In their language and in their manners there is even a certain elegance. Newspaper correspondents, who were scarcely friendly to us, made this remark in visiting our prisoners (a whole nation of soldiers), which such a monstrous chance has thrown into Germany. The Germans in France are quite different. Away from their own hearths, where they are excellent, forced out of their daily habits, out of that domestic idyllic life which deceives so many persons, they become at once rude and coarse. Thrusting them into a position, in which the inherent barbarism of their race, hitherto latent, has revealed itself, has been a great injury to them in public opinion. That which was below rose to the surface and was seen in its native hideousness. Oddly enough, it was not the soldiers who behaved worst; it was the landwehr; those peaceful citizens and fathers of families torn away from home and hearth by those French scoundrels so obstinately bent on defending themselves. It would appear that these good Germans would not have been guilty of such a folly. An English newspaper has cleverly and justly marked out that the most shocking part of the picture is that the rapacity was in proportion to the domestic affections. "I should like that watch for my son, who is at college; that gold chain would become my little daughter; what a beautiful silk dress! it would suit my wife; I will take it." During the morning hours there may be lucid intervals, but at night, after having been drinking all day, what is likely to be their condition? "We could never speak to the officers after five o'clock," said one, who had been with these armies; "they would not have understood us." This explains those requisitions of champagne by tipsy men in provinces where there is none to be had. They would insist upon having it, and be furious if it were not forthcoming.

All this was the repetition of 1815, which was as cruel, but less wantonly wicked. Then it was the revenge of all Europe on Napoleon I., the reprisals for so much blood shed by him. But there was no reason for it now. Had not the two people been at peace for fifty-five years? Another contrast is this. In 1815, it was the invasion of a people, a great national movement, a sincere and spontaneous and natural outburst. In 1870, all was foreseen, combined, prepared, directed by a cold but firm hand. All was arranged to inspire a vile terrorism.

Another innovation has taken place in this war, which makes it different from all others. It is the first time open towns have been bombarded; that houses beyond the ramparts have been aimed at;

leaving the soldiers untouched, but destroying the inhabitants, the families, the children, the women, so that their terrors should unnerve the soldiers and cause the surrender of the town. Bombs, shot, shells are not powerful enough for the conflagration. It must be stirred up and rendered inextinguishable by throwing on all the wood-work, the doors, the windows, the rafters, petroleum, which burns and spreads flames far and wide.

Europe, says an Englishman, seems to have retrograded several centuries. According to the code of civilized nations vessels in peril were aided and rescued even in foreign countries. Here the perilous voyages of balloons have met with no consideration or humanity. Their dangers have been terrible. One was lost in the ocean. Another carried by a whirlwind was caught on the peaks of St. Baume. That is not sufficient risk. They are fired upon. If the wretched aëronaut falls he is a prisoner. They do not fear to die, but to fall upon the soil of Prussia. "Heu, fuge crudeles terras; fuge littus avarum."

It is not war. It is destruction. From the point of view confessed by M. de Bismarck, it is not enough to conquer or to break, nothing must be spared, all must be destroyed. The privates acknowledge they could not have gutted everything so scientifically, they could not have been so thorough in pillage, so complete in devastation, but from their orders. Their officers have been told to teach them the Russsian method. The

Russians are masters in this art. Every part of the booty is arranged most methodically, in bags, boxes, trunks, and numbered to be sent off in such and such carts. In Poland, in the last century, the orders to carry away everything were so precise that three waggons were once found loaded with fragmentary dolls, which had been found in the houses of the wealthy. In 1849, the Russians in Hungary carried away everything down to morsels of broken mirrors. They had a line of carts which moved in one unbroken file from Pesth to the heart of Russia.

Do you think there is no account to be rendered for this? Do not think so. This is but the beginning. "War will *begin* next spring," said one of our soldiers the other day.

In one town our enemies experienced the energy given by despair. The imbecile municipality had disarmed the people. The town was nevertheless brutally assaulted by the outposts of an advancing battalion. An old judge died of fright. But the workmen, unarmed as they were, fell on the Prussians, and made them prisoners. The Prussian regiment arrived the next day, but the general so respected this heroic fury, and was so anxious it might not spread, that he obliged his men to pay for the pillage.

A Prussian officer said to a friend of mine,—a distinguished foreigner, whom I could name if necessary,—"We are resolved to succeed. And all is arranged and provided for us, to be three to one."

A cynical confession! Cannot you do better than that? Well, here, you will find men, and one to three will be enough.

Let me recall only this. In old days, when we invaded Prussia (men they were, without our modern weapons) our watchword was, "One to three."

CHAPTER X.

STRASBOURG.

NOTHING more clearly displays the spirit of revenge in the invasion, and its design of planting the seeds of undying hatred between the nations, than the employment of the Baden army for the destruction of Strasbourg. This barbarous work, actually executed by their nearest neighbours, makes Baden and Alsace mortal foes, and employs Baden as a Prussian gaoler, who has a personal interest created by his own crimes to hold fast his captive. But there is another consequence which has not, natural as it is, been provided for. The ditch between Alsace and Baden is, owing to this, immeasurably widened. The Rhine becomes, through these hatreds, fathomless. Between Strasbourg and Kehl at present it is not a river that flows; it is a gulf deep as an abyss, broad as the ocean.

How everything is changed now! We, in our blind sympathies for Germany, thought of Baden as such a pleasant holiday excursion. We considered the two shores identical, and many Frenchmen lived from choice on the German side, spent their money there, and lived there in those woods, on those heights, a calm, still, German life. All Europe came to it. It was like a neutral country, and agreeable to all. Here it seemed all nations could meet at the same table, shake hands together, and be friends. I remember that when this war commenced, a person who had been the first to protest against it wrote to the newspapers in favour of this pretty spot, the garden of Europe, being declâred neutral.

For me, I have again and again returned to those fair Rhine cities, especially its free towns—so well named free, and so dear to the friends of mental freedom. There is an amiability and sociability in them; they have not the heavy close atmosphere that belongs to the other towns of Germany. They are exuberant with light and warmth; they were bound to the free cities of Switzerland by the bond of a close fraternity. They were so friendly with each other, so neighbourly, these Swiss and German towns, brought so near by the "exulting and abounding river," that there is a homely proverb well known there, that "a dish baked in Switzerland is still hot when it reaches Strasbourg." Their connection with Holland and the Hanseatic towns is as intimate as with Switzerland. On every side Strasbourg, Frankfort, &c., were peacemakers between the nations. They had been the benefactors of the world by that great modern revelation, Printing. Their literature, light, sparkling, and satirical, is very different from the German. Mürner was a source of great amusement to me, and I am not surprised that the great Goethe, though born at Frankfort, pursued his studies at Strasbourg.

What an admirable place to live in was Strasbourg! Abundant in all commodities, in books, fulfilling all our needs. Studies, commerce, military life, were all blended there into animated and earnest existence.

The good old King of Bavaria, who was fond of the French, and received them hospitably, used to relate, in the early part of this century, what happy days he had passed at Strasbourg. It was a gay, warm-hearted kind of place, to which the frank simplicity, peculiar to Alsace, gave a primitive charm. But all was dignified and exalted by the warlike importance of its position, and by the lofty thoughts inspired by its monuments—the works of those great builders who have been imitated by the whole world. Here Goethe and Victor Hugo, poets, antiquarians, and artists, would come to draw inspiration and knowledge. The art of the Rhine is a school of itself.

If Alsace was stolen, as the Germans say by the French, they must acknowledge that she was stolen with her own consent, and was charmed to be so taken. There never was a more faithful marriage. How dare they divorce her so brutally! Let them consult her wishes on the subject! Alsace is France, and something more and better. The noble manufacturers of Alsace have occupied themselves more than has been done in any other part of France about the condition of the workman.

With its surprising power of production, Alsace has not occupied itself wholly with materials, but with man also. It has cared for human life. In war Alsatian heroes manifest the humanity which we think belongs to peace only. How touching are those notes written night by night by Kleber in the dreadful war of la Vendée! How much heart, how much human sympathy, we find in them!

But there is one stronger, more decisive proof of the filiation of Alsace to France, than any other; the great war-cry of France, which is called, I do not know why, *La Marseillaise*, originated here, struck out amid the burning national watch-fires which blazed on our frontiers, before the eyes of the enemy. This chant was composed at Strasbourg, and he who sang it was dumb after he left Alsace.

How generously Alsace welcomed that mass of German workmen, who were continually arriving here from their own country. 20,000 masons at least came every year from Baden to Mulhouse, Colmar, Strasbourg. They marked and observed the whole province, but were not friendly to us. They were enemies of the country which received them so well. The small cathedral of Friburg was jealous of that incomparable spire, which, from the Vosges to the Alps, points out the Queen of the Rhine.

The Duke of Baden, who was so cruel to his prisoners

in 1849, hated in them the friends of France, as well as the martyrs of liberty. It was not his fault that Floccon, our illustrious friend, did not perish for having betrayed the secrets of his prisons, sunk below the bed of the Rhine. His life was saved by the heroism of two Strasbourgers—his printer who gave him shelter and concealed him, and the agriculturist, M. North, who saved his life at the peril of his own. May that name live for ever!

General Uhric is now immortal. Abandoned, without artillerymen, having only infantry soldiers and a few Turcos, all know how he resisted the besiegers.

The King of Prussia's son-in-law, the Baden Duke, and General Werder, were cruelly inveterate. Even when the Swiss, sent by their cantons to entreat that the women, the sick, the old people, might be allowed to leave, these admirable missionaries of fraternity had, it is said, to enter Strasbourg exposed to the brunt of fire and ball, to fulfil their charitable task.

They obtained permission for a few of the inhabitants to leave; but the bombardment of the town went on, not so much of its walls and its citadels as of its most populous districts. Every one has deplored the irreparable loss of the library, and of so many other monuments. The damp unhealthy cellars of Strasbourg received a crowd of women, trembling under the rain of fire which, at night especially, fell on the roofs of the neighbouring houses with a terrible sound. The terror was at its height when the roof of the cathedral, an immensity of zinc, melted, and red and seething, illumined suddenly the whole town, giving to it and all the adjacent country an effect like a scene in the Last Judgment. This venerable monument, the loftiest in the whole world, sublime from the genius of its hero, Erwin de Steinbach, is dear to the people, because it was built by the people—millions of pilgrims, who each contributed their stone for the salvation of their souls. In its innumerable sculptures, it presents us with a complete world—angels, beasts, men, nature, and humanity. It marks a succession of ages. Near the choir, which is of Charlemagne's time, is the famous clock, a wonderful specimen of contemporary science, where the future revolutions of the planets are described. The statues on its portal suggest an infinity of thoughts. There are the foolish virgins in which we see the spirit of the old romances. There are also two strange figures sculptured by the daughter of Erwin: one is Christian Law, imposing and awful; the other Jewish Law, once so persecuted. The whole is the concrete mediæval life, the accumulated history of the world and of Strasbourg. These stones are an aggregate of human lives, piled up one over the other—human lives! nay, human souls!

In '93, during the Reign of Terror, these buildings were respected. The destructive impiety of kings was needed to attack this wonderful relic.

What is most extraordinary is the silence of the whole world as to these atrocities. The poor Swiss above mentioned, who exposed their very lives in the work of charity, excuse these deeds as well as they can.

Others have done more. What seems admirable *to them* is the attack, not the heroic resistance.

Fortunately, witnesses—earnest, single-minded, disinterested witnesses—abound. The most appalling fact is one related by a lady, who tells me (18th of October) something which had been passed over by all, as too shocking for belief. She asserts that these wretches, when they found their shot failing, maddened with their fury, to feed their guns, snatching up whatever they could lay their hands on, fired on the town keys, locks, weights, but above all stones, stones from the churchyard, the tombs of Strasbourg! They seized them from the cemeteries, and the terror-struck women, who fled from this ghastly hail, thought they had been struck by human bones.

My son, who died at thirty years of age, was buried at Strasbourg, in that friendly city. When shall I return there? Where shall I find his ashes? I know not. If they have been scattered about in that cruel chaos of marbles, corpses, biers, with which an impious fury thought to overwhelm us, it is well, those ashes will one day or another fall on the enemies of France!

CHAPTER XI.

GERMANY.

Is it true that there are already 29,000 widows in Bavaria?

It is certain that in this war the Prussians have largely made use of the blood of their neighbours. During the first terrible fight of Wörth they sent forth their Poles of Posen. At Gravelotte they again put forward their Poles to receive the first fire, and then called up their Swedes (I mean Pomeranians).

In the combats of the Loire, it was the blood of the Bavarians which was shed.

This is the result of the military treaties which they were all so hasty to sign in 1866 with Prussia; at the very moment when France was arresting Prussia on the Main, and was endeavouring to save South Germany from the pit into which Hanover, Hesse, Nassau, Frankfort had fallen.

But the unity of Germany? It had been more genuine and more true if Bavaria and the South had united in stipulating for themselves and the others sufficient guarantees. Poor deluded patriots! you who have betrayed the South, you who have cast it under the wheels of that chariot of iron which will ultimately grind your bones, learn one thing—unity may be the reverse of union. Do you call unity a grotesque alliance of conflicting elements within an iron circle, which binds, chokes, and smashes all?

But if not, you say, France would have destroyed us. What an astonishing ignorance of the times, the circumstances of 1866! Germans, Germans, ye who are so learned, are ye also so ignorant? Your eyesight is keen enough to distinguish, to specify the elements of the planets and teach us what are the metals in Mars or Saturn, but what is under your noses, what is so important to you, you do not even suspect it. France not only did not desire the war, but, as I have before proved, in the astonishing progress of her new sources of wealth, would have done anything rather than check the golden flow.

An aged infirm emperor, almost worn out with disease, was too preoccupied with his miserable Mexico to think of Europe. A resolute vigorous man would probably have gone, the day after Sadowa, into Germany, for the sake of German liberty, and to save Hanover, Hesse, and those wretched Bavarians. In that case, poor widows! you would not have lost your husbands.

But one thing was necessary—the utterance of that magic word Liberty,—" Freiheit "—although he speaks German so well—could not be spoken by him.

He waited, he procrastinated: a very prudent man—Niel—told him that before any action it was necessary to reform the army. Niel worked hard at it, but died in the middle of his task. His prudence and wisdom were, however, sheer folly. In spite of their needle-guns, the Prussian artillery had not been remodelled; and France, aided by Austria, by a sudden attack might have surprised the victors while they were plunged in their intoxication of success, could have snatched Hanover from them, saved Frankfort, preserved Bavaria and Suabia. In this case your poor wives, Germans of Munich, would not be all in mourning? And those black flags which I see at the windows, even during the illuminations in honour of your Emperor, would not sadden the eye and heart.

The mourning is in both countries: but there is this difference—yonder are husbands, here sons. Their loss is not in itself less dreadful; but, at all events, they leave no orphans.

Cruel result of ignorance and credulity; one word has maddened them—the word "Invader." But there are two invaders: before you is France, but behind is Russia.

And besides, Prussia is, after all, so little German—it is, in fact, a Slavonic state. Prussia, bound by a terrible tie with Russia, is the advanced-guard of Russia; your artisans have told you so.

Another lie of Prussia's to dazzle and fascinate Germany is this: "You are young, but they are old." The Latin race is effete, worn out; it has had its day.

This is the new birth of Germany, it is the day of Teutonia.

The Russians say precisely the same thing: "We are young, the Germans are old. Latin races and Teuton races are passed away; Slaves, it is the turn of Moscovia."

Germany is old, they say. Her enormous emigration proves it: she willingly leaves a worn-out land. She has shone fifty years through genius, literature, art; from Frederick to Beethoven, who died in 1827. Since then she has absorbed herself in erudition, in natural science, where methods are definite—where the line is so clearly drawn, that a mediocre capacity finds it possible to make discoveries. Tobacco, beer, and music have mesmerized them. Their *literati*, with their systems and discursive methods, are old. It is very necessary that our Prussia should wake them to actual life, and train them to those wars which will finally destroy Europe, and leave my path free. What they are now doing in France under our Prussian whipper-in, what they will do (in Austria, in Italy?) prepares our Europe. It is what in our science of destruction (the model of which has been Poland) we call the first operation.

This is an idle dream of Russia's. Neither France nor Germany are old. These great people have varying moments, ebb and flow, but infinite resources by which to renew themselves.*

* One word more about that folly so often repeated about the Latin races. Those who speak idioms derived from the Latin,

Who is young, and who is old? All these forms of language, borrowed from individual life, are absurd when they relate to nations. England was very old under James II., and older still under the Walpoles, and it was very young at the end of the eighteenth century, when it took possession of all the seas, made a vigorous start in industry and productions, and multiplied a hundredfold man's strength by steam and machinery.

France under Guizot was old. Afterwards, in spite of our bad government, she was young, full of promise and life, youthful in the Crimea, youthful in Italy. Yesterday she was becoming old again; but the sting of Germany has given her a new and ardent youth, terrible and full of rage. Paris displays it to-day, and all France to-morrow.

How blindly is Germany deceived! After the Prusso-Russian treaty betrayed by Russia (from the 1st to the 10th November), on the 26th the German Parliament voted for Bismarck, for the bloody dictatorship which now decimates Germany, and which will harness her to-morrow (*jumentum insipiens*) to the cannons of Russia.

---

are by no means Latin on that account. The majority of the French are Celts, with few Roman elements in them. The Spaniards are Iberians and Moors with the same scarcity of the Roman elements in them. Language deceives, it *does not* indicate race. The English are called Anglo-Saxon from their language, but they are a varied mixture in which there is much Breton, and still more Flemish and Dutch owing to emigration from 1200 to 1500.

Does not the insolence of Prussia, the arrest of your deputies, of Prince George of Saxony,—does not that prove your servitude? This bastard constitution, where those elected by universal suffrage have no power for peace or war, or for the fate of Germany. Is that enough? You have had five years of dictatorship, are you going to arm again the Russo-Prussian—arm him with the sovereign right of taking, without even asking, your purse and your children?

CHAPTER XII.

POSITION OF RUSSIA.

In 1851 a similar threatening cloud lowered blackly on us from the East. A chill and unhealthy shadow weighed on Europe. The government of that period, while preparing the 2nd of December, submitted itself in the most dastardly manner to the Czar. The Russian Ambassador had his seat in our Council Chamber. A friend said to me with intense indignation: "The Russian Empire reaches to Calais. I must go to America."

I steadily gazed at the monster which was approaching us, and I published a book, in which I expressed at once, my horror of Czarism, and my sympathy for these good, but unfortunate Russian people, who are like souls in purgatory, horribly enchanted in that Devil's empire, which has robbed them of life and development.

Those who could burst such a sepulture, break such an accursed spell, were heroes indeed. I have the sincerest worship for the martyrs of Russia, the Pestels, the Ryléiefs, the warmest fellowship with those intrepid writers, Herzen, Bakounine, Ogareff. Where shall I find a more ardent spirit than Herzen's (that genuine Iskander) whom I lost last year? What a brilliant mind! what light shone from him! He was the terrible truth-teller, who revealed Russia to us, sincere, not exaggerated in his testimony, perfectly agreed with the most earnest observers, the solid Haxthaüsen and all the most trustworthy witnesses. His paper, the *Kolokol*, an admirable specimen of true patriotism, manifests the noble illusions he sought still to cherish. Death struck him midway. New facts shattered his patriotic hopes. He has himself asserted, with an incomparable eloquence and fire, speaking of Pouschkin and others, what a power of extinction is possessed by Russia: how she kills every spring of life which flows towards her. How many people has she not extinguished. As a destructive force Russia is truly great. With how many lugubrious monuments, with how many sepulchres of nations has she covered the world. Poland will gradually be interred in Siberia, in those fortresses surrounded by the *tumuli*, which Peter the Great erected from the bones of the Swedes. The Caucasus, whose people were the chief of the white race for beauty and energy, is now a tomb. This exterminating frenzy, this fury of creating deserts (even without interest or aim) is so strong in the Russians, that in a space of a thousand leagues, it has swept away all those poor hunting-tribes who gave some life to the shores of the Arctic Sea. I have read this in the travels of two Russian engineers. All that side of our planet has become like the moon, an empty, barren, deserted world.

The worst of Czarism is that it is a religion. What a monstrous blasphemy to adore a living man. How did it arise? By the strong and terrible concentration it was necessary to oppose to the great deluges of Tartaric hordes. The fury of unity evoked an atrocious Messianism which deified a monster (Ivan 4th). Horrible incarnation of murder, hideous worship of death! It was sincere, though extravagant. We all have heard of that minister of Ivan's whom he impaled, and who, throughout his long agony, called out nothing else but "God save the Czar."

The Czar only is named in their form of worship. Loyalty to the Czar sums up their religious education. It is curious that Russia, in her opposition to Turkey, should say boldly, "I am Christian;" or that she should say, "I am a Greek against the barbarous Osmanli." How much would Prussia lose in passing under the Russian yoke. How much would the Slaves of the Danube lose also. The fearful recruiting of the Russian Empire must of itself give all nations a horror of this Moloch of the North. How much greater is the rule of Asia over her legitimate races than this Asia bastardised by its German bureaucracy, where two tyrannies are blended, that of the East and of Europe.

All true observers, Russians, and all, have said Russia is a Janus, a Proteus, a changing mask, an immense lie, a world in which everything has a false sparkle. The celebrated emancipation of the serfs is an aggravation of Czarism. It is singular how Americans and others have been deceived in this.

This faith of Czarism had lost a good deal of its prestige after the Crimea. The god had sunk very low, and was deeply in debt. A great stroke of fanaticism re-enshrined him and repaired his finances. The 240,000 men who make the Russian nobility (minus the women, children, and old men, for then there are 900,000) are officials, or sons of officials, ancient dignitaries of the empire. A decree of Peter the Great's father, who made the peasant a serf, created the property of these officials. Peter made it, Alexander in '61 unmade it. He suppressed the screen (this pseudo-nobility) which these puppets of the Czar held between him and the serfs. It was a great scenic clap-trap. The Czar-god, who hitherto had dwelt on high, comes down upon the altar, and says, "I am here." This living god says to the serfs, to those 50,000,000 corpses, "Arise! Live!" If this nobility yet exists and keeps half its lands, a certain primacy, as it were, it possesses this primacy for the sole purpose of being odious to its inferiors, so that the Czar can always *pose* as the protector of the serf.

Our good Czar, who defends us, who bestows on us our land, how can one bless him sufficiently. Remark two things, however, that in relieving the peasant from the claims of his landlord, the Czar charges him with an equivalent burden to increase his own imperial revenue.

He has more than doubled the direct taxation (*vide* Wolowski). The twenty million of peasants who, for a long time since Alexander I., had been made free, and styled the free peasants of the crown, found the imperial functionary much harder than the landlord had been. This functionary at this moment has power throughout the empire to elect or confirm the mayor (starost) of the commune. In proclaiming with a great flourish of trumpets the free commune of Russia, it is not added that the Czar, after all, is absolute over it, for this starost, elected and chosen by him, is his puppet.

Herzen! Ogareff! My dear friends, what a blow was this fact to all your poetical dreams. Herzen, with his admirable and warm-hearted enthusiasm, said, "Our new symbol is bread." The landlord will no longer eat the bread of the poor peasant. That is true, but it is the Czar who eats it, doubling, trebling the tax on it.

The false purveyor of the people, the socialist tyrant whom I have so often pointed out in the cities of antiquity, returns to us here with his mask. It is a vast comedy, which makes the admiration of the world. "The commune is re-established, free elections are re-established, the jury, the provincial parliaments—there is nothing wanting; England, America, are nothing beside it."

Do you think this can hardly be? I swear to you these are their phrases.

Alas! when I find that in England elections are

bribed, purchased, the sifted jury of France such an idle mockery, you would make me believe that the Russian peasant, degraded during two centuries, that man whose own wife and daughters were not absolutely his, that man who could be beaten like a hound, could be changed at once into a free elector!

Elector? he will elect whomsoever the functionary of the Czar chooses. Trial by jury? the functionary will tell him whom to absolve, whom to condemn. All is an idle ceremony. The true title of this new liberty, is tyranny.

The error which we in Europe commit, is to suppose that against this internal revolution, a certain stifled resistance on the part of the nobles can occupy, embarrass, or paralyze Russia. It is an erroneous supposition. This imperceptible people of nobles is null in action, senseless from fear. It lives, if it lives at all, as a grace, on its knees. Does it live? No. The only living person in Russia is the Czar, in whom is concentrated the strength of all the masses below him—fifty or sixty millions of human beings, who are nought in themselves, but who live only on him! Will they ever be men? Possibly! But now they are only a huge force, a steam-engine. Can they be permitted to repose? That fearful unity which they acquired yesterday, must it not be employed?

Of herself, Russia gravitates to the west and the south. That is her natural motion. She is most mobile. She has been delayed, but she will recommence her march. Through Bohemia and its party of fools, she will have a door open into Germany. On the other side, Prussia, in spite of its little passing attempts at enfranchisement, will only be able to keep down Germany by opposing to its recriminations and its claims, the fear of Russia.

The destruction of France, which struck the blow of the Crimea, the destruction of Austria, which had shown, timidly enough it is true, some disposition to favour Poland, is the one thought of Russia. To accomplish this, M. Bismarck has been a most excellent instrument.

During the Sabbats of Biarritz, when the tempter obtained from the sick man a bond against himself, Russia stood by, observing her agent. That sepulchral spirit, whose eyes, hidden by impenetrable glasses, have never been seen—that Spirit named Gortschakoff, watched the other at his work.

Did he not manipulate too well? The victory, the violence, through which Frankfort, Hanover, so many more provinces, were crammed into a bag with outcries so vehement, shows the double position of M. de Bismarck. To silence the Germans, he promised them the Baltic and gave them his favourite toy, universal suffrage, and a constitution without guarantees. To console his king and satisfy Russia, he proved how easily and without any danger he could lend himself to the farce. "The Baltic? those ports? that navy? Do you believe, my dear friends, I am serious?"

A stranger who, at that time, dined with Bismarck and the Russian Ambassador, witnessed a curious scene. There had been, up to this time, a cloud between the two diplomatists, but that had passed away, and they had drawn together again. Such reconciliations, even when secret, are always agreeable. But this went on before numerous witnesses, and there were soft and meaning glances interchanged, covert yet tender allusions; in short, it was quite a diplomatic idyll. The observer felt that under all this there must be some new agreement; that such a mutual understanding threatened some horrible misfortune to the rest of the world. He did not breathe a word to any one, but he shuddered. Attila was fond of jokes. History has preserved some of them. There is a recent one (November, 1870) which is not a bad one, according to the taste of a Hun, and is, besides, seasoned with a leaven of half hypocrisy, or rather mockery, which gives it additional zest. The Czar admires Germany excessively. He aspires to a citizen army, to possess patriot soldiers. His ideal is the landwehr, "a good defensive army." Therefore, to his 700,000 men, he adds a pretended landwehr of 500,000 more.

All this is to make a promenade towards the Bosphorus to the mouths of the Danube. Here he will find a Prussian. Then it will be seen if the Danube, according to the vain promises of Bismarck to his patriots, is a German river.

That which the Russian people hate most in the world is a German.

Against France and the West, Holland, England, an agreement has been made which is now revealed.

But a compact with death is not without its dangers. How will M. de Bismarck settle with his fearful ally?

At the final catastrophe of the Sabbat, Satan, who had promised to his children all the good things of this world, and this world to each, to fulfil his word, had one decisive method. He disappeared in a flame of fire . . . Ask the smoke, the air, what had become of him!

CHAPTER XIII.

FRANCE AND EUROPE.

I HAVE written this little work in the darkness of December, while a shroud of snow covered all Europe. A gloomy winter, in which the old glacier period seems to have again fallen upon us. Few or none of the nations who were our friends have raised their voices for France. Are they asleep? We might believe it. Paris closed and dumb since September, has since then known nothing of the living world. Its noblest voices have been heroically closed, walled in by themselves. It is the oldest, perchance the weakest of them all who now speaks. He, at all events, has been enabled to see and observe.

One fact has struck him very much, the indefatigable pains which have been taken to hide the struggle in night, or at least to conceal it with false lights. It was a bold plan, by which the victors sought to win over and to intimidate the European press.

It was a species of chloroform, through which, by means of cheap newspapers, countries which thought themselves most wide awake were set to sleep. By a certain drowsiness it is easy to detect the commencement of that disease which I will call the Prusso-Russian-influence. It is like the cholera.

On the principal routes, on the Rhine, on the great thoroughfares of the world, a vast net-work of police was organized to detect and check all communication. The effort was vain. What Russia in her Cimmerian darkness could do to her prey, Poland, was not to be done in the broad light of Europe.

Now, on this 1st January, the day dawns. In spite of all, certain warnings are heard on all sides.

They seek to keep us in the dark. I will try to bring the light. In spite of themselves they shall see.

The Prussians are entirely ignorant of France. The false details of their innumerable spies flattered them into thinking they would find in France an easy prey. How often they have been deceived!

After all, nothing is more foolish or more deceitful than a police report. In '53 the Emperor Nicholas found himself caught by one. His principal spy, the old and clever Princess L——, was consulted on the question, "Will France dare to make war?" She consulted some *doctrinaire* high priest, who answered, "France dares not." From this answer arose the senseless bravadoes which brought down on Nicholas the great rebuff of the Crimea.

This time their inquiries, their secret emissaries, all their police, their treachery, sedulously employed for four years, gave them a thousand exact details; but a collective view, which, as a whole, was entirely false. The kings who came to the great Exhibition of '67, believed in the moral dissolution of France, and took their own private advantage out of it. They judged it by the actresses and the farces of Offenbach, to which they themselves were so eager to hasten. In '69, seeing the political storm, noting our sudden uprising, they said, "Now is the moment."

My dear friends, you reasoned badly. At such moments of waking, whatever may be the partial dissensions, whatever may be the government, be it the worst in the whole world, a people is very much to be feared.

Learn that in '69 France was overflowing with life—was rich in strength, in full-blooded emotion, in a fierce tumult of joy, which centupled that life. The Socialist movement, which gave *you* hope, was entirely local, and confined to certain populous centres. Our dissatisfied workmen were not the less, as you can perfectly well see for yourselves to-day, ardent citizens, and, if needed, intrepid combatants for the unity of France.

How is it that you ignored on what a mighty anchor rested that ship which seemed to you so tempestuously agitated? The great peasant people—at once our anchor and our cable—never had a stronger basis than now, having recently, especially in the South and West, become proprietors—independent proprietors. This, of course, binds them to the *status quo* of Peace; but that very fact also makes them firm, proud, and invincible, when the soil of France is touched.

You are beginning to learn it, and you will learn it more and more.

I am wonder-struck to see how utterly France is misunderstood and unknown.

That some of her special faculties should be ignored, a certain electricity which is at times her saving grace, and at others causes those fiery outbreaks and unexpected recoils which are each mighty enough to shake the world —that these should be ignored, I can understand. I know that the most illustrious geniuses of other nations have not the least idea of them. But what is a simple fact, which he who runs may read in five hundred histories, law books, statistics,—even almanacks,—how did you come to overlook it, ye Germans, with all your wisdom, reputed so great?

Go to your books of natural history, of physiology, and endeavour to grasp for once the meaning of these words,—*Organic Unity.*

It is the unity of one nation,—of France.

It is the unity of a people incapable of being dismembered;—of a national body whose circulation throughout is so rapid and complete that no separation of its parts can take place.

In this respect all that you have still to seek for, we already possess. We possess *identity of law* from Flanders to the Pyrenees; and this not at the period of the actual legislation, but by a process of concretion going on slowly but inevitably for centuries—the work of legal science. We possess *administrative unity,* that instrument of Colbert, imitated, though clumsily, by so many nations, and which, though occasionally ill-used, has been only too powerful with us, and serves as a guarantee for a national personality not easy to change. We posses a *unity of circulation,* solely the work of these last twenty years,—not only by means of railways, but of roads, and a thousand other ways altogether new;—so that the life-blood of Languedoc or Provence may in a moment be found coursing through Alsace. Cut out this? Good heavens! you might just as well try to cut out the veins and arteries of the human frame. Dismemberment signifies death!

A matter of extremely old date, and one altogether peculiar to France, is the singular completeness with which the *fusion of its races* has been accomplished and its various populations intermixed and welded together. How far away is Germany from this yet! How many years will it take to convert that fiction of unity which you have been trying to vamp up within these last few years into a unity like ours! Tell me when will the Prussian be loved by the Bavarian. I will answer you—"Never." The great memories of the past, the grand traditions held in common, the military *esprit-de-corps* which pervades all France, have drawn more closely and strongly our ties. Our forefathers have fought, suffered, and often perished together. The same spirit animates their sons.

One very singular fact in it all is this, which also proves, how in material, moral unity is included, the

Provinces, which seem at first sight to have been inhabited by different races, and who speak dialects which are not French, are precisely those which are most French at heart. Brittany, which has a language of its own, is not the less the rock, the primitive islet on which France is built. Lorraine, through Joan of Arc, is our sword; through many others also of our brave soldiers, need I name him who covered with his body the retreat from Moscow?

It is Alsace, our valiant Alsace, great both in industry and war; it is Strasbourg, as I have before said, which inspired that glorious hymn in which dwells the true soul of France, generous, peace-loving, magnanimous in the fiercest strife.

That is our Unity, let us see that of others.

Suppose the Fenians succeeded to-morrow in snatching Ireland from England, will any one say that owing to that the English Unity would be broken?

Suppose that Catalonia was separated from Spain, I should regret it for the sake of that fair realm of loosely-bound provinces, but it would be more like breaking a bundle of rods than severing an Unity.

The glorious Unity of Poland was genuine in that sacred Empire which has so often saved the rest of Europe. Yet when the Cossack province broke away from her, it did but follow the natural tendencies inherent to it. Lithuania itself, which gave to Poland so much genius, through which the spirit of Poland has revealed itself to the whole earth,—dreamy Lithuania, had a life of her own, which set her somewhat aside from her brilliant sister.

At the same time, moral unity, however imperfect, seems to me priceless in all nations. I have never wished that that fatal left bank of the Rhine should be added to France. Though Germany is so little homogeneous, though to-day her cruel link of iron is but union, I should think it impious to make the Frankfort of Goethe, the Bonn of Beethoven, French. They are essentially German.

But let our neighbours permit me to say to them one earnest and sincere word.

To dig out Alsace and Lorraine from a living body, from the strongest organic unity which has ever existed, to dig out these viscera with a knife, to cram them into a body like Germany, which is in a state of formation, would be a strange surgery. Oh self-deceived, why would you spread slavery, give serfs to Prussia, the ally of Russia, the advanced guard of Russia? Leave those men to France, you will need her soon.

In 1815, in spite of the Prussians, Europe had rejected the idea of the dismemberment of France, but in 1870 was not at all averse to it, and found it natural that Prussia should seize her Eastern Frontier, that France of Alsace and Lorraine, without which the exposed centre is thoroughly insecure.

In 1815 Europe was comparatively moderate, after so many evils, so much bloodshed, which must have exasperated her. In 1870, after fifty-five years of peace, she approves at once of the strange claims, the inexplicable fury of Germany, who had suffered nothing from us as yet, and yet who affirmed without a shadow of pretext :—" I will tear away a limb from that trunk, I will cut my pound of flesh near to the heart."

These enormous reprisals for the wrong which France *might* have done, but had not done, seemed just and natural to our neighbours and friends, to whom we had just opened our markets, who lived on our commodities, and for whom France is a milch cow. The small states, menaced by the neighbourhood of a military government, and vexed by its police, like Geneva, were much more excusable. But in general in all the nations the hatred was more in proportion to the jealousy and envy they felt for France, than relative to the injuries France might inflict, which she had not done as yet, but of which they were constantly afraid.

Every one said, " It is the fault of France, she began it ; " no one would remember the violated engagements, the continual provocations of Prussia during four years, the military *espionage*, the officers, the engineers, detected taking the plans of our fortresses, &c.

Poland was sad. I am assured that the Poles of Posen showed a great reluctance to fight against France. Therefore they were sent to Wörth, to Gravelotte, wherever the fire was most murderous.

Denmark was sad. She remembered that France had stipulated for her that Schleswig was to vote freely. A stipulation which Prussia trod under foot.

Switzerland was at first favourable to Germany, but was not the less admirable in her wisdom, her charity, her disinterestedness. She refused the aggrandisement which Bismarck offered her generously at our cost.

He offered portions of France to all the world. He sought accomplices everywhere. Italy refused him also, justly embittered as she was against those who had so long deprived her of Rome.

There was the same resentment in America, on account of the secret understanding of the Empire with the Confederates. America recognized the Republic, but injured it by sending some of her great generals to the enemy's camp.

America and England had been cleverly operated upon. The latter, at the moment of our disaster, offered a strange spectacle. Her ministers took refuge in the country (as well as the Queen, whose sympathies are pardonably Prussian of course), that they might not know anything, might not have to answer anything.

In England there was a good deal of methodistical bitterness among the higher classes against Voltairian France. It was piously expressed by an English writer in the *Pall Mall Gazette*, 15th December, "What a revolting sight," he said, "to see criminals who have been conquered, refuse expiation." They do not thank Prussia for chastising them and helping on their salvation, and are so hardened and ferocious," added he, "that the poor Germans might be assassinated if they should enter Paris."

The correspondents of Bismarck, who travel with him and dine with him, exaggerate these animosities by cowardly sneers, fabulous news, giving the most sarcastic pictures of Paris which they could not see, and which from the 19th September was invested and closed. Suddenly there comes a lightning flash—the Russian note of the 1st November, a dry sharp sound is heard, such as is made by a mitrailleuse, and "Jean qui rit" becomes "Jean qui pleure." What a grimace! what a grotesque and demoniacal play of muscles in the abrupt and spasmodic laughter caused by this note. But England herself was not with these buffoons. She paused. She did not smile. She seemed to wake, and saw herself facing the white Bear, alone. She called out, "Where is France?"

At such a moment how strongly one feels that each of these great nations is necessary to the world, and what an awful eclipse it would be if one perished. What would be the desolation, the horror of the rest of the world, if one morning we heard England was wrecked, submerged! Even that rabid Germany itself, who against her own interests is so inveterate against us, if the Baltic overflowed her, how deeply we should mourn. The European sentiment is gradually rousing itself. Those who thought they did not like us, who were afraid of the Empire, or jealous of France, now experienced a sudden and fraternal reaction. This was especially manifested by the warm-hearted Belgians, and in a most tender and touching way.

We can scarcely read, without tears, the zealous, violent transports of charity which they evinced in seeing our wounded, and in receiving, almost disputing, for their possession. The surgeons had never seen anything like it, and will never see it again. Neighbours quarrelled which should receive the wounded. One said to the other, "While I was away you robbed me of my wounded guest. Give him back, if not——" And they would actually fight, as to which should retain the mutilated man.

There is one hero in Europe. One. I do not know two. His whole life is a legend. As he has the greatest reason to feel animosity towards France, one knows at once that with his nature, that man is going to devote himself to France. He is a great man. My one hero. Loftier than any present fortune, how his sublime pyramid of glory grows towards the Future.

How fine a history will be written one day of the noble Italian hearts who made so many efforts to follow him! Neither the sea, nor the horror of the Alps in mid-winter, arrested them.

What a winter! Never was a more severe one. In a snow-storm which lasted several days, and obstructed all the passes (at the end of November), one of these heroes would not be turned back. Through the horrible deluge he obstinately ascended, from station to station. The thunder of the avalanches could not arrest him. He pursued his way, opposing to the snow, which was freezing him, the vital forces of his passionate, invincible heart. Pierced through and through with the cold, covered with icicles, by the time he had scaled the height, he was one mass of crystal. The tempest was over, and all was over for him also.

He had passed away. He was frozen to death under that blue arch from which one sees France. There he was discovered. No clue was found by which he could be traced. All the newspapers mentioned him, but none knew his name. I can reveal it. He who so nobly rushed to France in the hour when all had deserted her was called—Italy.

Let us here, however, mention some of the generous words which have been spoken for us by the English at this moment, and which forcibly declare to their nation what help she owes her suffering ally.

The illustrious Lord Russell and a number of Englishmen have, in their different newspapers, spoken admirably for us and for their own country, which is so deeply interested in our fate. But no one has expressed himself with so much force, vigour, and logic as Mr. Frederic Harrison, in a memorable article (*Fortnightly Review*),—an article which I consider an important national fact, and which remains as a written witness of the profound communion which exists between the two great nations of the West.

In it he deplores the retrograde strides which Prussia in this war has forced upon Europe. Europe has been put back fifty years. The war has a character peculiarly its own. The wars of the first Empire were wars of impulse and headlong courage, rash, and not coldly premeditated. He acknowledges, what few will acknowledge, that the unexpected defence of France is something striking, heroic, such as no nation has made under such reverses.

"What she has lost in material influence, she will gain in moral. Around her will gather the peoples, all the Republicans of Europe. Her sufferings will give a new impetus to the cause. Henceforth we feel that the French people, even in the eyes of the German Democrats, bear the banner of Progress."

The same writer affirms, which is also proved by their great meetings, that English workmen have felt the greatest agitation at this noble spectacle presented by France, and they display their sympathy, in spite of the efforts made to neutralise its effect. They do so in spite of so many unworthy journals, on whom Prussian and aristocratic influences weigh so heavily; in spite of the moneyed classes, so infatuated with peace, that they would insist upon it were war in London itself; in spite of their own interests at stake, the lowering of wages, these operatives judge, with much good sense, that if England loses her place as a power, her trade will not merely suffer, it will be lost.

Moreover, there is a natural perspicacity in the English, which makes them often thoroughly just. Every one must have been struck by this in the cotton famine of the American war. In their meetings they always voted for absolute justice, in the teeth of their own interests.

If the honest artisans of England had, like those of Germany, some prejudices against France, they have now abjured them. They have seen that, under an apparently trifling exterior, there are in us both moral force and true dignity. Where has one seen at such a violent crisis such a revolution, uniting so much gentleness to so much grandeur? In Paris, in that multiform ocean of two millions of men, no bloodshed, no violence. The socialist agitation, the ardour for battle, which caused *one* day's outbreak, were not the less humane. At Lyons, one man perished. It was a great misfortune, for it gave an excellent excuse for the abuse of our enemies. One man! It is, of course, too much: but when one has traversed, as I have done, an entire history, so many bloody revolutions among the calmest peoples, it is all but miraculous to find that only one man perished in the tempest! One only, during all the violent exasperation in which we were thrown by our miseries! One only, among the many known traitors and spies!

What a power has this republic obtained immediately and without effort, for security of persons and property! The civil power commands; the military power obeys. It is a strong frugal government, which costs the people nothing. With what regularity the taxes necessary for the armies engaged to save it are paid by this people!

All these facts will make English workmen and people of all countries reflect when they contrast them with the patent treasons of monarchy. In France, it betrayed the army. In England, how often, in times past, it has betrayed the honour and safety of the people. Dynastic alliances and relationships make kings and queens an ominous family, whose interests are apart from, and often against, those of their subjects. This is why Charles I., the kinsman and friend of the enemy, refused to interpose in the Thirty Years' War. He forgot the claims of English honour, and looked coldly at the death of two millions of men.

The Crown and the Shop have acted in harmonious agreement: their organ, Mr. Gladstone, says to the people, "Mind your own business." "But Russia insults us; our vessels are fired on; nay, the letters of our Government are not forwarded, but detained at the pleasure of Bismarck." "Mind your own business." "Is not the safety of the country the business of the greatest importance; and when we have let go Holland and Belgium, and when Prussia has the iron-clad fleet of France,—when you see them land,—where will our shops be?"

It is certain that Paris by her long resistance has saved, in one way, France, and that France, by resisting, saves Europe. The marvel is how, with those new legions, so young and ill-prepared, it has been possible to retard and thwart those great experienced armies, the standing army of Prussia, that deluge of a million of men which Prussia poured on us. That our Mobiles, leaving the plough, the loom, the counter, the office, should have marched against this nation of soldiers, even though they have been defeated, is utterly admirable. Defeat like that, under such circumstances, is of itself a gain. It has made Europe reflect. Heroic defeats on the path to victory!

Yes, Europe has admired; Europe has been touched at the unequal struggle. Those sublime boys, marching against those old soldiers, against those engines of death, so wonderfully constructed and so minutely calculated to do their work,—marching, and being defeated and killed. The earth is younger for their blood. It has bloomed anew.

It also speaks of our divisions. Where are they? Some think—friends and enemies—that we are *weakened* by dissensions on social problems, that we are verging on civil war. That is a mistake—our very excitement makes us not weak but formidable. The passions of '69, the rages which burst forth on us, popular ferment, all have taken a new course, and with a power which a people not stirred up beforehand had not found in itself.

Now, the awful scourge which evoked that strength, serves and increases it. How? It is as in '93. We are lighter; we are purged. We have cast out Imperialism and its systems. We have put aside the old Adam, profligate expenditure, idleness, a great assemblage of costly vices, which were uppermost yesterday. The workman is armed, the peasant is armed. Emulation is universal. No distrust. Let me explain why.

With the equilibrium she has, France can face the social question.

Our intelligent workmen know the situation perfectly. They see beside them their natural balance—a million of peasants. "Respect the peasant," said Bakounine, in his recent pamphlet; "respect his field, his orchard. If you touch them, you perish. The agricultural majority, at the least fear on that head, would elect, ten times over, your tyrant."

Our workmen know France, and with France, Europe. It is a benefit for her that they see her as a whole and on all sides. They, like the German and English workmen, had very acutely judged the question of the war. They will judge equally well the commercial question. Knowing perfectly the European market, the price at which each people can produce (under risk of losing the capital), they will only desire that which is possible. That sense of fraternity which in these late events has so revealed itself in them leads me to think that they will become more and more co-operative, and that their co-operations will enable them to produce more cheaply, making competition day by day less useful and rarer. Therefore, the social question touches us, but does not alarm us. The new revolution will simplify it. That will happen which always happens after such overthrows, that in the enormous activity which succeeds them work and workmen obtain a sudden increase of value. Capital is in search of Labour, as Mr. Harrison says well. The rich man, who has only his wealth, and who runs the chance of its remaining useless and unproductive, depends on the man of true wealth—I mean him who has the handicraft and the productive mind, on him who creates. The capitalist, in other words (by an admirable reversing of ordinary society), is the client of the creator—the banker is the client of the workman.

A great lesson is taught by this vast shipwreck. The social question must harmonise with the higher, nobler question of freedom, or all will perish alike. Our country itself, preoccupied by the first question, and too much absorbed by it, we slipped into the abyss. Our fall was watched.

But the more deeply we fell, the more buoyantly France, as she touched the ground with her feet, upraised herself and again ascends.

It is a blessing for all. She alone, by her singular strength of equilibrium, planted on her strong basis, can await the tempest, and, organizing the world of labour, defend even her enemies, by arresting the march of yonder giant masses which are darkening the horizon.

THE END.

LONDON:
PRINTED BY SMITH, ELDER AND CO.,
OLD BAILEY, E.C.

www.ingramcontent.com/pod-product-compliance
Lightning Source LLC
LaVergne TN
LVHW021415110826
845150LV00007B/1939

* 9 7 8 1 4 2 5 5 1 0 0 3 9 *